THE RICH VAULT OF LORE

EXCLUSIVE TREASURES OF VALUABLE KNOWLEDGE

Copyright ©: Richard Darklyn Ofei
Independently Published: Richard Darklyn Ofei
1st Edition: 2021

All rights reserved. No part of this publication may be reproduced or transmitted in any form or by any means, electronic or mechanical, including photocopy, recording, or any information storage and retrieval system, without permission in writing from the publisher.

The author has tried to trace and acknowledge sources/resources/individuals. If any information is incorrectly attributed or credited, the author is pleased to rectify these omissions at the earliest opportunity.

ISBN: 978-0-620-96526-2

Written by:

Richard Darklyn Ofei
rdarklyn@gmail.com

Table of Contents

Dedication iv
Introduction 5
1 Unveiling the Mystery of Keys 7
2 Friends, True Friends & Relationships 11
3 Managing Friends Whilst In a Relationship or Married 19
4 Evolution of Relationship 29
5 The Swot Analysis of Relationship 42
6 Toxic Friendships to a Relationship & Marriage 49
7 Meant to Be or Not Meant to Be 55
8 Understanding Your Partner's Perspective 61
9 Thinking About Your Ex 69
10 Kindling Romance to Ignite Spark 74
11 The Concept of Age in the Choice of a Partner 83
12 Recipe to a Healthy Relationship & Marriage 88
13 Mr Right & Mrs Perfect 95
14 Are You with Mr Right or Mr Right Now? 100
15 Attraction Magnets of a Union 104
16 Physical & Emotional Intimacy 109
17 Your Moral Compass 120
18 Love Personified 131
19 Why Relationship Fails 136
20 History of Marriage 142
21 Honouring Your Partner 147
22 Phubbing 152
23 "Creepy Love" Gender-Based Violence 157
24 Ancient Proverbial Expression of Wisdom 166
Conclusion 173

DEDICATION

Firstly, let me thank the God Almighty for inspiring my thoughts to the discovery of "The Rich Vault of Lore". I dedicate this book to my wife (Faith), my precious daughters (Solace & Jasmin), and to all who aspire to have a successful lifelong relationship, friendship, and marriage. Lastly, a special dedication to the victims of Gender-Based Violence.

The keys to a successful relationship are treasures embedded in a secret vault of our hearts. They are required during the life cycle of our human relationships, courtships, and marriages to nourish a happy life on earth.

Richard Darklyn Ofei

Introduction

The Rich Vault of Lore is inspired by a constant quest for a relationship that can withstand the trials and storms of life. We mistakenly assume that our perception of the world, is the way the world is supposed to be. When our partners and friends disagree with us, it's easy to conclude that they have a distorted perception of the reality of life.

Failure to understand that different people are entitled to their point of view is a grave failure to appreciate our differences. Our perspectives of life need to be respected and valued at all time, to ensure a sustainable relationship. Our values and beliefs create our world and they affect our opinions, behaviours, including our perspectives in relationships. Understanding the true composition of relationship with a disciplined attitude, is a gateway to discovering new ways of understanding your partner's point of view.

The recent crimes of Gender-Based Violence against humanity are a call for an in-depth understanding of life and issues surrounding relationships. The fact that most of Gender-Based Violence crimes are committed by close associates, family, and supposed love ones, is a real indication of our misunderstanding of the essence of relationships. The misunderstanding of relationships and value for humanity is one of the integral source of the untold abuse and the killings of women in situations that could be avoided.

A relationship is an inevitable part of the human race. It is common knowledge that every individual requires some kind of stability in his/her relationship. Therefore, this book is written to accommodate different categories of people and belief systems; to draw attention to issues of critical concerns that will empower the society.

You may have all the material possessions in this world but in the absence of a committed, trustworthy, and lovely relationship with your partner, friends, and family, your life will be a wreck. The evolution of relationships, friendships, and marriages into rocky status leading to painful breakups and divorce is a concern that is valued by *"The Rich Vault of Lore"*.

Relationship and marriages are orchestrated by two individuals with a common goal, which is to love each other. The tango between these two individuals in the long term brings together a community of friends and family from both individuals in support of a union that breeds a spirit of love and unity to the overall benefit of humanity. A relationship, friendship, and marriage born out of true love are epitome to a collective unconditional peaceful human coexistence.

On the other hand, a sour relationship, friendship, and marriage can exacerbate a storm of misdemeanour among people to a tsunami of war, affecting every facet of society and life. It can lead to untold destruction of a family, community, and an entire human race. It is against this background and other noted concerns that this book is coined to include certain pertinent elements that if well understood and articulated in practice, could lead to sustainability; devoid of the emergence of chronic pain and hurt that wrecks potentially wonderful unions.

1

UNVEILING THE MYSTERY OF KEYS

Keys and locks were invented to protect valuables. The interpretation of what valuables are differs from one person to the other. And what is of value today might not be of necessity tomorrow. You cannot gain access to a house without a key. With the right keys, you have access but whilst in the house, you may only have access to particular rooms by the use of other keys. Once you gain access to a room, you are only able to open wardrobes, cupboards, trunks, and safes that contain valuables by the use of keys. It is seemingly clear at this stage that one key cannot singlehandedly open a locked house, room, wardrobe, trunks, cupboard, cabinet, safe, etc.-, successfully at a go.

Like a house requiring different keys for access to its different compartments, human beings require different keys in the form of certain pertinent attributes, characters, behaviours, actions, and treatments to unlock different aspects of their being. Our organs and body parts respond differently to different situations and times.

The only way to gain access to a house and its other compartments without the right key is, by the use of a force; unauthorised entry (break-in). In which case, the intruder commits a punishable offence and could be subjected to prosecution. An unauthorised entry causes pain, damage, and suffering to the property owners for their hard-earned assets.

You may steal somebody's heart with all the wrong keys. You may enter into somebody's life for acceptance by false pretence. You may portray an act of kindness with ulterior motives, just to gain acceptance for love.

Whichever method you try to use to gain entry, chances are that you may indeed gain access in the end through perseverance and a bit of luck. If you do not have the right keys (genuine character, true intentions, and good attitudes among others) for entry, your only means for access will be by false pretence and awful deceit. You can have a relationship with anyone at any time through the tactics of force pretence. But the deceptive lure of entry without the necessary key attributes to a person's heart will expose you badly sooner than later.

Keys are raw metals until modified by locksmiths, and tailored to open specific doors. Human beings also are mere living entities and therefore require the consistent effort in self-development built on humanly accepted moral values to shape a person to become the embodiment of another person in friendship, relationship, or marriage. A good locksmith is required to shape and beat metals to specifications that fit the requirement of specific knobs or locks. A good man or woman is equally required to cultivate and exhibit genuinely selfless attributes for acceptance into the bosom of a forever-lovely relationship and marriage.

Men and women are the metals and the fruit of their human nature are the keys that define them. It's worth noting that access to another person's heart, body, and soul needs time. This is because time is the only element that will pave the way to understand the person you have your mind fixed on before further commitment. Knowing the good and bad sides of a person makes it easier to make a choice, and assist in dealing with unforeseeable circumstances. It is not easy to know the whole being of a person at a go, because our human environment and series of events affect behaviour over time. A bit of an effort with patience will arm you with valuable signals to make an informed decision. The golden keys to a successful relationship and marriages are sharpened during the early stages of a relationship, and are used before commitment in a relationship. It is imperative to note that, every door requires specific keys to unlock and that the idea of a master key is a myth.

To identify the right keys that can open doors and sweep-off the feet of your partner, it is necessary to exercise patience in humility and understand the real nature of your potential partner. Remember, the keys you used years back to win the heart of a previous partner, may not necessarily work on your current or future partner. The keys your friend or neighbour used to attract his/her partner may equally not work in your situation. It is important to treat every person as a unique individual Keys have been baffling ever since I started sorting through an old collection of them; as I try to figure out their use and why I still have them around. I may have travelled with some of them for years from places I have lived before. Some of them look like car keys but not one I own now.

Have you ever found yourself in a situation where your bunch of keys has a particular one not in use? Yes, it happens to most of us. The keys not in use may be keys for other doors or locks not in use at the present moment, but you still hold on to them for known or unknown reasons. It could be because you think they might be useful for another lock someday. You could also be having them unconsciously and will throw them away immediately you become conscious that they are useless.

You should be able to leave the past where it belongs and never carry the burden of all the wrong keys into your next relationship. It is important to turn a new leaf, identify exactly what will make your partner happy, and do it with good intent. It is not bad to emulate and apply good marital principles from other couples or friends but be sure they are compatible with your situation and that of your partner. Forcing your partner or friends to behave, act and live like other people to please your ego will just blow up in your face.

We are uniquely made and things appeal to us differently. Whereas going to the movies will be a romantic and appealing venture to one partner, others may despise it and will rather opt for an early morning jogging together. If you have owned a key before you will also note that, it has some little bumps. Upon insertion into a lock, the little bumps lift a series of pins inside the lock.

The lock is only able to open if the bumps on the key lift the pins in the right manner. Inaccurate bumps that do not match the configuration of the pins will result in an inability to open. Similarly, you need to present yourself and possess attributes that fit the emotional, physical, intellectual, and social needs of your significant person. If you don't fit and encounter difficulty, don't force, exercise patience in perseverance to grow towards the direction of acceptance.

Just as you may be patient enough to go back to a locksmith to resize your faulty keys to a door. Remember that each relationship has the potential to be a lock and fit to open the way for a good life. There is nothing pleasant than accepting and being accepted in a relationship by a person you look up to. It is vital to remain patient when in a relationship or marriage, so that you do not force your way out to get things done according to your desire, at the expense of your partner's wishes. Forcing a relationship ends in the same fashion as forcing a key into a lock.

When you stay in a relationship or marriage for a long time battling the frictions that come your way, you at some point have a feeling that your love or that of your significant half lessen. In such instances, you must restore the pinnacle of your love union to an active mode just as you fix a worn-out key to continue its operation of opening doors without struggle.

"I feel that as long as you're honest, you have the opportunity to grow. It's when you shut down, go into denial, and try to start hiding things from yourself and others, that's when you lock in certain behaviours and attitudes that keep you stuck."

Tracy McMillan

2

FRIENDS, TRUE FRIENDS & RELATIONSHIPS

Friendships and relationships are two similar but distinctly different situations that are often misunderstood, misconstrued, and confused. Friendship is a relationship between two or more individuals who do not depend on each other for making decisions. Relationship on the other hand, is the status of two individuals who depend on each other in decision making.

The subject of dependency is in fact what differentiates the two. Individuals in a relationship are not always free to make their own choices without considering the plight of the other partner because they have to be mindful of what is best for both partners.

Friendship is usually between people of the same sex or people of the opposite sex, but romantic relationship is among people of different sexes, although the current adoption of LGBT+ gives access to same-sex romantic relationships. It is possible to have a friendship without a relationship, but relationships that are not based on friendship cannot stand the test of time.

From a comprehensive standpoint, a relationship comes in two forms: the natural form and the deliberate form. Biological family members are natural relatives but one can also enter into a relationship by a deliberate conscious means. Aristotle, a Greek philosopher, and scientist once said, "Wishing to be friends is quick work, but friendship is a slow-ripening fruit." According to him, friendship can be classified into three different categories:

- *Friendships of utility*
- *Friendships of pleasure and*
- *True friendship*

Friendships of utility are instances where people are on friendly terms for the benefits each brings to the table, such as schoolmates or workmates. In most instances, persons in this relationship submit to the relationship for specific gains. People of this calibre of friendship disappear or starts to misbehave after their needs are met.

Friendships of pleasure are those instances where people find each other based on what the enjoyment the friendship brings. Examples are people hanging out due to similar hobbies or common interests. This friendship dissolves when the reason for pleasure no longer appeals to the parties. A typical case is a partner who professes love to another for material gains or sexual pleasure.

True friends on the other hand are friendships based upon respect, appreciation for each other's qualities and a strong will to aid and assist each other due to the recognition of each other's greatness or ways of life. Such friends are always available and ready to go the extra.

The first two types of friendships are easily broken because they are driven by a person's mere utility and pleasure. They fade off as soon as benefits are achieved. However, friendship based on goodness is long-lasting and referred to as "True Friends". They are the kind of people you can be intimate without worrying. They are the people you can share experiences, memories, and promises with; the kind that neither time nor distance can break apart. According to Aristotle, It is also possible to have all three friendships in your life.

Take a minute and critically examine your circle of friends. You will come to a shocking realization that some of your friends are only there because of something they gain from you. And there will surely be a likelihood of those who only want to be around you during times of fun, and of course, the amazing ones who might be there in good and bad times. It is said that he that finds a true friend finds a priceless treasure. The emphasis is on a "good friend". True friendship is unconditional and can stand the test of all odds, leading to an irresistible passion of two souls transforming into perfect couples.

When marriage is formed from a sustainable unconditional true-friendship, garnished with a selfless forever love and draped in care and kindness, it produces an unbreakable bond and a happy family union. Marriage was designed to meet the need for our companionship.

The first time God said that something in his creation was not good was at the creation of a man: He said "it is not good for the man to be alone." God's intention was that the man needed a companion in the form of a woman to complete him. This is therefore not to say that everyone needs to marry at any time with just anyone in order to be complete. It does not also guarantee that marriage will be a ticket to meeting all our needs for companionship. Since God is the designer of marriage, it is therefore safe and correct to say that it takes 3 to make a good marriage: ***God, Man, and Woman.*** In other words, to fulfil our need for companionship; marriage needs to be a primary, permanent, exclusive, and intimate all-round relationship. Ignore the needs of one of the three (3) and the bond will be in shamble gasping for oxygen to survive.

The relationship of marriage is nothing like the parent-child relationship we know. It is therefore very important for everyone to alter the parent-child relationship through proper upbringings before moving to the point of establishing a deep relationship with a partner leading to a holy matrimony. This is a direct confirmation that people with bad parent-child upbringing have greater chances of struggling in their relationships. Marriage does not automatically mean abandoning parents or guardians for a life partner. A person needs enough emotional maturity before breaking away from parents' dependency for a marriage. One must be brought up under the tutelage of responsible parenting, positive community influence, and upbringing in order to be responsibly equipped as an independent adult. Being a good husband to your wife and a good wife to your husband is the only sure way to be good parents to your kids. Marriage relationships are required to be built on commitment rather than a feeling of romantic love. Commitment is the pillar that holds couples together through unforeseeable difficulties that are sure to force their way into relationships by any means possible.

Feelings on the other hand are like smoke that evaporates in no time regardless of its thickness. Romantic love cannot stand the test of difficulties that invariably rears its ugly heads during the cause of a marital relationship.

The Transition from a Friend Zone to Committed Relationship Status

I have come to a simple but acceptable conclusion that the easiest part of a relationship is falling in love. What is challenging and neck-breaking before dating is, finding compatibility, trust, and commitment in a person. It becomes even more difficult if the person you are falling in love with happens to be your friend. It is highly possible to transition from just being friends into a committed dating relationship leading to marriage. But this transition requires quite a load of prior to an engagement to avoid risking an already existing friendship. It is awkward to profess your feelings to a friend only to be turned down with the usual "I like you but can we rather remain friends." As a result of the painful turn-down effect, one has to be very retrospective of a friendship. Do a thorough introspection before taking a step towards the relationship zone. Ask yourself questions that will lead you to realise whether this person feels what you feel; whether you can remain friends with this person if his/her answer is contrary to your expectations. Find out about signs that confirm if this person might also be interested beyond the "friend zone".

Before attempting any move, be sure that your friend is also blowing some "positive winds" your way in the form of touching, regular eye contact, and notable signs of flirting. Many people find it difficult to transition from a friend zone into building a romantically connected and sustainable relationship for different reasons. Some friends get hurt when they are left out by their friends when it comes to choosing a partner because they would have wished to be chosen.

The following will assist you to break the friend zone and transition into a serious commitment with ease:

Show That You Care Beyond Mere Friends

Transitioning from a friend zone to something sustaining requires you to prove that you care more than a friend would. One of the best ways to show how much you care is, identifying a need that your friend will so much love to meet. Make a strategic move by surprising him/her with provisions to that need in the form of your candid appreciation of the friendship. Meeting a person's need have a way of bringing you closer to the person and it even creates a stronger bond. You will be closer to hitting the jackpot to a heart you have been dreaming of if the person is your close friend and the good deed was done in sincerity without the attachment of unnecessarily selfish strings.

Share Your Hopes, Dreams, and Future Aspirations

We sometimes get over ourselves thinking we know someone better only to realise that we only know that which the person wants us to know because of the friendship. If your intentions are pure then you have to take bold steps to engage in deeper conversations with your friend regarding the future expectations and what it holds. An iota of revelation on the part of your friends regarding their willingness to settle down with a partner and whether they aspires to be a wife/husband with kids in the future will give you a realistic idea of whether the person in question is in the game of sourcing for a partner or not. The ideas of talking about a potential future with friends have a magical way of clearing up misconceptions to develop the path for further bonding.

Exercise Patience

Remember, the mere fact that you are friends does not mean you have a license to become great partners. It's one thing being a friend and a completely different game to be considered a committed romantic partner with the possibility of being a wife or husband.

Allow your relationship to grow at a reasonable pace without unrealistic expectations. Being patient is the only way to win the race at its natural pace.

Discover Clarity on How He/ She Feels About You

Knowing how your friend feels about you is the first step to knowing whether a move will work in your favour or backfire. Take a step only when you are confident of his/her feelings towards you. In that case, you will increase your chance of hitting the jackpot to a wonderful heart. Sometimes you may think someone loves you due to a certain action, only to realise at a later that the act you misconstrue as love, was just passive and nothing sustaining. If someone likes you in a situation that could lead to something more than friends, then you will usually get feedback and reasonable invitations to connect on a different level.

Avoid Making Sex a Foremost Priority

Under no circumstances should sex be a drive to communicate your affections.. That could be the greatest turn-off and might ruin your chances of ever discovering the beauty of that heart. Rushing to have sex with a friend you expect to become your significant half is an indication of bad and selfish intent. Your friend might even think that you are only sexually attracted to her. Remember, sex is not the hallmark of a relationship, and a man who prioritises sex instead of trying to know his woman better is up to no good.

Your Intention Must Be Indirectly Made Known

This is where you are supposed to create social awareness of your genuine feelings for him/her indirectly. You could make use of both physical and emotional compliments to express your utmost desire. It's important not to overdo it because he/she might be a foreigner to such moves of compliments, and it may feel or look awkward.

Make sure that you don't leave room for assumptions because that can put both of you in an uncomfortable situation going forth. It's best to ask questions, but be realistic and stay relevant in questioning to avoid offending him/her. If you handle these points appropriately, you will have a greater chance to succeed in being accepted for a relationship. There is one of two things you should be cautious of in the process though. Since you have been friends for a while, chances are that he/she may have told you about him/herself.

You may have heard or seen him/her with the opposite sex, probably in a compromising situation. In view of that possibility, you owe yourself a responsibility to lose the jealousy and not unnecessarily judge him/her by the past. One of the most important things to do during the transition period is to discuss what you both want so that you can remain on the same page. The whole intent will be a flop if one person wants a fling and the other is expecting commitment.

Therefore, understanding the long-term needs and desires of your partnership will clear the path for a mutual understanding. None of you will end up being hurt or disappointed. It's not fun and easy to have such conversations but it is surely the most appropriate thing to do for a great and healthy beginning. Just as you know a bit about him/her and probably about his/her other friends and those he/she might have been interested in while you were still friends; he/she equally knows a bit about you and those you might have been cosy with in the past. Don't be afraid to express your thought and feelings about what you know but do it with the right intent and the sky will only be your springboard to a greater height in a mutually fascinating relationship.

"The greatest happiness of life is the conviction that we are loved; loved for ourselves, or rather, loved in spite of ourselves."

Victor Hugo

3

MANAGING FRIENDS WHILST IN A RELATIONSHIP OR MARRIED

Relationships are a very important part of our lives. They often give us meaning, purpose, positive emotions, and contribute to our sense of well-being. But they can sometimes destroy some of your greatest friendships. Friendships can come between people in relationships if care is not taken to manage both ends. The "happy ever after" statement concerning marriage is a myth. In fact, for a relationship to work, you need to put in time and effort regularly, making sacrifices elsewhere in your life. After marriage comes a complicated effort to manage yourself, your partner, your friends, and the environment around you. This task requires extra effort, commitment, and wisdom to realise the happiness and success you aspire to.

If you choose to rather be with your friends most of the time rather than with your partner, then maybe you need a second look at who you are in a relationship with and why you are in that relationship. It is healthy to sometimes feel like spending time with your friends but that does not mean sacrificing the joy and happiness of your partner. Friendship and relationships are two separate entities and they should be seen and handled as such. Spending time with friends is not a taboo in a relationship or marriage but it should not take precedence over the time you spend with your partner. There's nothing wrong with meeting friends and occasionally spending some time together but there should always be a limit. If you focus on making a relationship work by giving it the time and energy it deserves, then you may have to give thought to how much time you spend with friends. It is worth acknowledging that being married does not in any way disqualify one from having friends.

Spending time with friends without your spouse can be nice but it is important to recognise the potential danger it could create for your union. If times spent with friends begin to take precedence over time spent with spouses, it could become a dangerous habit that can lead to infidelity. While you may be innocent of wrong doing, your spouse may not appreciate the time you spend with friends, especially the opposite sex. The people we spend most of our time with are the greatest influence on our lives. And while having a friend is important for personal development and growth it can also offer too many unnecessary voices and opinions that will in the end become a recipe for distraction and complete disaster. Notwithstanding, it is necessary to have trusted, intelligent, and open-minded friends whom you can look up to for sound advice to help in treating your spouse with love and consideration.

Naledi confronted Jasper about a female friend, and his response was, "Don't you trust me?" Jasper's interpretation was that Naledi doubts his integrity. A lot of spouses respond to such situations in a similar or same defensive approach. You either take the concern personally or shift the blame to the other person calling them jealous, paranoid, or control freaks. This blame submission rather leads to further frustration that disconnects the relationship. It could exacerbate fighting that might cause more damage than good to the relationship. Couples need to sit and have a decent talk and possibly set some positive boundaries for peaceful relationship. Study your friends and stay away from those that do not have the moral values and ethics as yourself. If you surround yourself with negativity and drama, then that is what you will produce. You will in no doubt take it to your relationship or marital home. But if you surround yourself with positive people, then you are sure of good counsel. Remember, negative people are like a wedge within a marriage. They are up to no good as they cause instability and confusion. Unfortunately, there are people that exercise happiness when others are in a misery.

Such calibres of people are very good at convincing others to believe whatever they say as the truth. Subjecting yourself to lies will only cause a rift within your marriage or relationship. Investing valuable time with someone who has no intention of bringing anything positive into your life will put unnecessary strain on your relationships and marriage. Married people should at all-time rethink male/female friendships. The concern with clinching to male/female friends without boundaries is a big threat to many people. The reality is that, the more you are attached to a person, the more you want to know more about them. The more you get to know a person of the opposite sex, the greater the chances of developing bonds. Whereas this can be healthy between people of the same sex, it quickly transitions into unhealthy attachment between people of the opposite sex. Women in particular, sometimes lose track of how powerful they are over men. Women can have normal conversations with men without realising that their action and inaction is speaking a different language to men. A man may have a wild assumption that a certain woman wants something more by reading from their level of attachment. Be informed, several things can divert a man's heart to a woman's attentiveness. Ironically, the woman may not have invested thoughts into whatever feeling the man will be aiming at. Women, in particular, are not in any way responsible for how men thinks, but they should undoubtedly be sensitive to their level of friendliness; the number and length of time they spend talking to other men.

Continuous unrealistic engagement with the opposite sex can create a source of dissatisfaction with your partner. When you choose to make friends with the opposite sex, you don't experience the dilemmas that come with a committed relationship and marriage. It is easy to begin enjoying the company of friends because the relationship is casual, fun and there is often nothing of a serious nature to discuss. With time, you will be tempted to discuss your relationship or marital issues with such friends, and that is where problem arises. The most likely thing we discuss upon meeting with my friends is soccer.

We are usually busy with outings during specific times on the global football calendar especially World Cup, AFCON, UEFA Champions League, and the Premier leagues. Being a die-hard Barcelona fan, the champions' league season is always a good time to discuss soccer with friends who support other clubs in the English Premier League. A whole outing can be unconsciously dedicated to discussions around a pending game or that which has already been played. It will be difficult doing the same with the opposite sex. Because we are humans, our sinful nature sometimes causes us to do what we don't want at certain times.

There is a scripture I remember so well from my primary school days which I recited in one of those year-end school functions, *Romans 7: 15 " I do not understand what I do, for what I want to do I do not do, but what I hate I do"* (For I do not understand my actions. For I do not do what I want, but I do the very thing I hate). I honestly had no understanding of the content as it was a mere rhyme to me then. As I grew up, I came to believe that Paul was cautioning us in that passage to never underestimate our sinful nature.

You are at liberty to have friends of other genders, but don't be fooled to think you are above cheating on your spouse if you are not careful. You should not by any means let your guard down with a man other than your husband and a woman other than your wife. The caution here is not in any way adopted as a strict rule to prevent people from talking to men or women beside their partners nor is it about setting unimaginable boundaries that will make one behave weirdly towards people of different genders. It is a signal of caution about toxic male/female friendship or relationship outside your marriage or committed union. There is no new or old friendship that is worth damaging an already existing one especially those of marriages.

Essential Qualities of a Good Partner

You may have heard about this "wife material" term but I doubt if we talk more of a husband material. Interestingly the qualities that make one a wife material can equally qualify a man as a husband material or otherwise. In most cases cooking, cleaning, doing laundry, and staying home is used to qualify a woman as wife material. In as much as those are elements worth considering they are no strict qualifications for wife materials. Women are not created as agents of domestic work and therefore, require much more qualities than the ability to do house chores to be considered a worthy wife material. Whether your partner can fulfil the duties of a wife/husband or not is a question only you can have an answer to.

Since you will be spending your entire life with your partner, it is of utmost importance that you take time to assess him/her before further commitment. Commitment to marriage is one of the personal biggest collective decisions you'll ever make in life as couples. Look out for some or all of the following signs as decisive elements prior to accepting or offering a hand in marriage:

Self-sufficient*:* a good relationship requires mutual support from both partners. Those who can take care of themselves physically and emotionally are partners worth relying on. If you fall for a person that cannot take care of them-selves, you are literally inviting a child to your home. You will have to sacrifice to become a nanny to that child indefinitely if you want the relationship to see the light of days ahead.

Efforts to make you a better person: A person who inspires and motivates you to be a better version of yourself is a person with qualities to look up to. If you are likely to find a friend or partner doing everything possible to improve your career, health, and home life, they are much interested in you, and commitment to them will be a great choice. Not everyone have genuine interest in the success of other people.

You will see yourselves as competitive partners to outperform each other on a daily basis if you do not possess the spirit of trying to make each other better in a relationship. Such unhealthy competition can lead to unimaginable fall-out and essentially create fertile avenue for abuse. A partner with your best interest at heart will support anything that will shape your life and dismiss those with the potential of degrading your life. Look out for this quality because you wouldn't like to settle with a person who will be filled with pain and jealousy at your progress. A person who does not show effort to make you a better person can sabotage your success and even sacrifice your relationship for anything in the future.

A person that follows through*:* A person who lives up to their promises and does what they say is fully committed to a relationship. Beware of promise and failed partners. Ignore people who exhibit these traits of character from the days of dating before committing your heart and soul. Living with a person that does not follow through will leave you with a life of regret after commitment or marriage. There are people who generally over-promise and under-deliver in relationships. This trait cannot be hidden by anyone and a careful evaluation of a potential partner's lifestyle and communication can reveal if they are people that follow through or not. The impact of broken promises is catalyst for toxic relationships and must not be ignored or underestimated. Sometimes, doing exactly what is promised isn't possible due to unforeseeable circumstances but a chronic victim of these attribute will repeat the action with a lame excuse multiple times. Beware of people who over promise or make impossible commitments because they always have a hidden agenda that only benefits them and not you or the relationship.

Ability to handle change: Change is inevitable in any facet of life but some people get into a relationship thinking things are going to be just as they were from the beginning. A person that understands change and can manage that which comes his/her way is matured enough to adapt to new circumstances and situations that will affect the relationship with time.

Whether you like it or not there will be changes in your lives as time progresses. Changes could come in different forms and shapes. There will be good ones to celebrate and not too good ones that will throw a challenge to the strength and survival of the relationship. Either way, it takes persons with the ability to handle change to be able to survive. Divorce happens between people who ones live a life of struggle from hand to mouth when they are suddenly blessed with wealth because of inability to handle and manage the change. Couples who lived a wealthy life do also fall-out when their financial stability is challenged. Some families develop toxicity when children becomes part of their lives and others live a life of hate and name calling leading to sever emotional wreck when delayed with the gift of having children or it absence thereof. In all these and many others, it will take the ability to handle change to withstand and remain committed to wither the storm. A partner that cannot handle change will jump ship at anything abandoning you at the time you need them the most.

Ready to be your best friend: You have to be with a person you are comfortable sharing your life with, both the good and the bad. A person whom you hardly survive with as a friend will not magically become the best of a couple to you in the future. It is common knowledge that people are always comfortable around their best friends and will share anything from success to failure without any negative judgement. Your potential partner should be a person from this category because you will be one and one means one. You are going to share a life together and therefore should be able to remain friends even after marriage. Marriage should not override friendship but rather complement it to a fulfilling end. Imagine being with a partner whom you cannot discuss common issues with because you cannot simply reason along the lines of friends. If you are unable to sustain friendship or a potential partner cannot be a best friend then your relationship will be a master-servant relationship. A master-servant relationship is tantamount to abusiveness that will get worse and breed unhappiness as you progress through the different stages of the relationship.

Have a plan for his/her life: A person with a plan of where he/she wants to see themselves is worth considering. Have a plan for everything because he/she knows planning leads to successful accomplishments of goals and objectives. Don't be fooled into a relationship with an unorganised partner who only does things on the go. Planning is essential for the success of every relationship and if you don't have plans for your own life, how do you intend to handle or accept other people's plans or better still that of a relationship? People often overlook this important aspect of their potential better half and it always comes back to bite them. A person without a life plan will not understand your plans and cannot be a support to lean on. They will become a liability and in order to hide their shortfalls will eventually become control freaks. You can't just wake-up and make impulsive decisions without planning because the decisions you make affect not only you but your partner.

A person that makes you part of his/her life: A partner who is eager to make you part of his/her life and doesn't mind introducing you to close family and friends is a real deal. Anyone that sees you as a potential long-term partner will make it a goal for you to become part of their life. A friend who brushes discussions relating to commitment and marriage is not worth considering as a partner. The result of all relationships is marriage; therefore the person who shows no intention of making you part of their life is only with you to satisfy a selfish end.

This is where abuse in most cases rears its ugly head to badly haunt ones lovely partnership. What will be the most genuine reason why a partner will not want a significant half to be part of their life? Your partner is not comfortably introducing you to the people or things in his life, but will sneak in and out to have intercourse with you. A person who does not share their dreams with you does not see any future with you and not worth your commitment.

Good sense of humour: It's healthy to have a long-term relationship or marry a person that makes you happy and laugh most of the time. Laughing together as a couple is healthy for a relationship.

After all, laughter is considered the best medicine to overcome stress. A partner who can find humour in little things even after disagreeing with you is the type that can handle the shocks of married life. This does not mean that, you should be on the look-out for a comedian. One does not have to be a comedian to exhibit a sense of humour. Displaying a sense of humour should also not be confused with making expensive jokes that may cause pain and frustration to the other. A person that uses humour as an ice-breaker and social lubricant will be able to create a relaxed atmosphere for the resolution of problems and reconciliation. Whilst trying to discover the sense of humour of a potential half, make sure you look-out for the one person that can laugh with you and not at you.

Not a party animal: A partner who can have fun outside the club is a material worth considering than the one who is always at the club over the weekends and sometimes during the day. A partner who is always drunk can hardly take care of a family with kids and greater responsibilities. It's worth having fun but the one who is always present at a party or function will certainly not have time for commitment and the upbringing of children that might be blessed with the partnership. You will find it difficult to change a party animal into what you want them to be instead of what and who they want to be. Your effort for a change will be a highway to getting painfully dumped in the process. If you can set aside time to think about what you require in a partner and identify the signals that might not compliment your needs and values, you will be on a path to a happy choice and union.

The problem is that, we often underestimate triggers that should serve as a warning to reconsider our decision for relationships because of lust or love misconstrued. Understanding the actions of people prior to commitment will avert most cases of abusive relationships due to making wrong choices. People don't just change; it is the environment that changes. People's inability to cope with change reveals their real character and attributes with time.

It is not easy to hide a bad habit from a relationship and not easy to hide a good habit too. The signs will always be there to be seen by those who want to see. So look-out and make a choice that will not haunt your happiness and progress. Your decision to consider someone as a partner is a choice and not a matter of chance or sheer luck.

"A friend is one that knows you as you are, understands where you have been, accepts what you have become, and still gently allows you to grow."

William Shakespeare

4

EVOLUTION OF RELATIONSHIP

The Basic Interpersonal Communication Theory states that all relationships have a beginning, middle, and the end. Usually it takes something extreme for a relationship to end, such as setting a boundary to never see or talk to someone again or worse of all, death. There is no end to a relationship than evolution because relationships simply change from their usual form to another. With time, interactions and bonds tend to be different than they might have been, but they are still there. Loving someone is a continuous decision we need to make each day. Love is therefore not something you just fall in and out of when it suits you. It is something you need to engage into consistently in the right way so as to taste and feel its goodness.

I have told people over the years that I don't fall in love and they sometimes get surprised. I believe that falling can be accidental yet accidents can cause injuries. With love, it will be an injury to the heart. I believe in growing in love. This gives me enough time to analyse situations and grow gradually with the person in question to a point of emotional and physical attachment and innate conviction of acceptance. I am always able to deal with anything that comes up during my adventurous engagement to find love. Growing in love is much difficult compare to falling in love, but it's the best between the two. When you grow in love, you transcend personal differences in your beliefs, thinking, values, and aspirations of life and you work out a common goal towards a fulfilling relationship. Your heart will be hardly broken if you grow in love because you are not blinded by the infatuation that gives rise to falling in love. Growing in love impacts positively on your self-esteem and you can handle whatever comes your way without bruising your ego and self-esteem if the relationship doesn't work.

Being accepted or rejected by a person you seriously need as a significant half can bring mixed reactions of joy and pain, depending on whether the outcome is in your favour or not. One thing you should never give away regardless of the outcome of your adventurous engagement in a relationship is your self-esteem. This is because falling in love cannot guarantee it. Falling in love and receiving a negative outcome can break your heart and self-esteem. Growing in love on the other hand, could give you heartache yet will leave your self-esteem intact; making it possible to heal quickly, remain relevant and become healthy enough to carry on with your life. When you grow in love, you give yourself time to develop and disappointments are handled gracefully.

This explains why some people either mourn a fallen relationship longer or remain bitter for the rest of their life. Others carry on with their life as normal within few days or weeks after a break-up. There are times that you will become frustrated that your relationship is not what it used to be. You must recognize that a position of misunderstanding and changes in certain aspects of the relationship does not mean you have come to the end or approaching a break-up. Rather, consider the relationship as simply evolving and find ways to remain relevant in the changes that come your way. Understanding and embracing the evolution of relationships will build patience in you to find means to ensure that you do not make a hasty decision to prematurely end it all. Embracing change is not the most exciting thing to do for some obvious reasons, even in establishments. But the most successful person is the one that embraces change and manages it to a logical end. Change is the only constant in life. The possession of essential keys for successful relationships will give you the authority and confidence to withstand all forms of evolution in your relationship. We often aimlessly spend much of our time in anger, thinking that our friendship and connections aren't what we want them to be when we should rather be spending time to discover how much we have evolved with time. The most logical thing to do at the time of change is to find ways to embrace the change to make room for means to maintain and kindle the relationship.

When a relationship evolves from a mere acquaintance, friendship to intimate friendship and possibly marriage, we seldom consider it a bad thing. This is because we like the change in terms of the extra time spent together and the emotional or erotic benefit associated with it, and more importantly the fact that we may be with a significant half at last. We become completely ignorant or easily forget that such emotional benefits and the goodies of a found love also come with associated responsibilities and that it's not always going to be as rosy as the beginning. Until the relationship proves to be beyond repair amidst chronic physical or emotional abuse, being able to understand and manage change will reposition you to an ecstatic blissful state. Couples need to get better at navigating relationships because change doesn't necessarily signify an end, but a call to adopt and remain significant for a continuous partnership.

I asked a friend of mine why he broke up with his wife and he said Richard, *"We just grew apart, changed so much since we got together, and we didn't have anything in common anymore, "she isn't whom I thought she was."* It's quite normal for couples to go their separate ways when they are no longer on the same path, lack of growth, or their choices tend to be conflicting. These changes signify an important opportunity for both parties to step up and explore what is underneath the discord; bring about a healing that would initiate a new dawn and deeper level of love. It is of priceless honour to experience working, developing, and growing together in a relationship. There is so much that can be appreciated from learning through commitment in relationships and its evolution. But we are often eluded by other things and refuse to see and embrace the change holistically. There are three distinct sides to every relationship; *you, your partner, and the relationship* that you both created by what you bring to the table. As we evolve, our contributions to the relationship also go into a state of change. If a partner is not moving in parallel with you, the relationship will become unbalance and subject to hit rock-bottom through frustration.

Evolved relationships do not call for an immediate dissolution, rather it involves accepting the change and recognising that things are not only different but will continue to be different. Managing the differences in the relationship and your differences as individual couples in a relationship is the only way to build a strong bond in synergy. The preceding five essential keys are pillars that if well mounted in a relationship will lead to inevitable success through stability:

Key of Compassion

A meaningful relationship has compassion as its central point. Partners imagine themselves in each other's shoes when the need arises to ease the pain of another through understanding. Relationships are one of the most fulfilling moments in our lives. They can also challenge us beyond our human comprehension. We need emotional intelligence in our bid to build a sustainable and successful relationship. I learnt this aspect of emotional intelligence the hard way through a young lady friend from Ukraine. One of her cats was diagnosed with kidney problems by the vet and it unfortunately died shortly. My emotion to the death of the cat was short-lived, while she got so engrossed into mourning it for as long as she could. My response to the death of the cat did not meet her expectation. She saw through me and said, "Richard, your emotional intelligence is questionable". I got offended at why she could rate my emotional intelligence as low as she did by the fact that I couldn't mourn the death of her cat enough as she did. It was only at a later time that I reflected on what she said and realised that I could have done better. The death of a cat may not mean much to me but that doesn't mean it meant nothing to her too. Putting myself into her shoe and being emotionally intelligent enough to understand her pain could have gone a long way to ease her pain and develop our relationship even better.

Having a level of emotional intelligence enables a person to remain living with their partner even when they aren't able to effectively communicate their needs.

Most people enter into a romantic relationship to enjoy decent partnership and yet, when misunderstandings arise and they aren't feeling connected with their partner, their default mode is to quickly lash out or shut down another. To overcome this and to avoid sabotaging your relationships, compassion as a major component of emotional intelligence is your one-way ticket to saving your relationships. Seasoned psychologist, Abraham Maslow in his theory of needs outlined that, all of our behaviours are driven by our needs; our needs are derived from our emotional states. After our needs of food and shelter have been met, we also have very important basic needs—four of which are the need for attention, affection, appreciation, and acceptance. How you seek these things is dependent upon our level of emotional intelligence, our beliefs, and our core values.

Key of Humility

Studies show that humility is a quality that can help promote successful relationships. This may sound simple because it involves only sacrificing self-gratification to meet another person's needs. However, it could be hard to accomplish at the same time because it does not come naturally as we would have wished. When issues arise in a relationship, people with humility are more willing to listen to understand rather than listen to react. You will agree with me that humble people do not have any major drive to be right when confronted with neck-breaking issues. Those with humility are more likely to accept a point of view other than their own and they usually have less of a need to lobby their spouse or partner to see things their way. It is imperative to note that, if one partner acts selflessly and the other partner exploits them by acting selfishly, the humble partner loses out and opens door for frustration. Some relationships have one humble person who is consistently 'giving,' and one selfish person always 'taking.'

This can lead to a periodic tension that can result in one of two things: *long-term emotional abuse* if the selfless partner can't pull away or *a relationship that is headed for the gutter* sooner than later. "My mother warned me about this before I got married to her," said Jabulani in a frustrating comment to his wife. These are not the words you want to hear from your partner during an argument. David and Sheila have been married for twenty years. I admire them and their enviable relationship that has stood the test of time. Sheila refused to allow their son (Tim) to visit David's brother at the homestead during the summer school break. It was just a simple talk that disintegrated into an argument due to misunderstanding. Needless to say, they both ended up in one of those hours of deliberations. It's not that they yelled or said anything hurtful to each other but they just got too exhausted mentally and gave up and walked away from the conversation, emotionally disconnected. David remained calm in humility and encouraged Sheila not to give up or feel bad about the pattern of expressing their opinions on issues. Sheila was against the visit for fear of her son staying with an uncle who is hardly home to keep an eye on her teenage boy. David on the other hand wanted Tim to bond with his cousins as a family.

After tempers had calmed down, David heeded Sheila's reasoning and agreed not to allow Tim to visit the homestead without them until he is a bit older. During conflicts, a prideful heart is mostly self-consumed and cannot see beyond its thoughts, opinions, perspective, pain, feelings, and needs. Humility and grace are the keys to turning conflicts into something that benefits relationships and marriage. Conflict serves to bring partners closer together, rather than further apart if handled from the angle of humility. At the end of the day, couples in argument interestingly seek the same goodwill just with a seemingly different approach. You can agree and disagree while remaining humble to seek a solution for reconnection. Conflicts in intimate relationships tend to be expeditiously dealt with only when individuals can humbly acknowledge their respective shortcomings and think about their partner's opinion too.

This allows relationships to repair effortlessly leading to deeper understanding and improved emotional bonds.

Key of Gentleness

The trunk of an elephant is a particular source of strength coupled with precise control. It has more than 40,000 individual muscles and is strong enough to rip branches from trees but equally sensitive enough to pick up a single blade of grass from the ground. Gentleness is seemingly a strong hand with a soft touch. It is a tender and compassionate approach toward other people's weaknesses and limitations.

A gentle person can speak the truth, sometimes even painful truth, but with a guarded tone for the truth to be well received by all. My daughter loved hitting me on the chest when I carry her probably trying to make it hurt. She could hit with all her might, but it never hurt. She didn't need to be gentle because she lacked the power to cause me any pain. Then, just for fun, I would put her down and punch her chest with a fist until she laughs. It's the strong hand (mine) and not the weak one (daughter's) that must learn to be gentle. Harshness might make someone obedient or compliant, but gentleness wins the heart. Some people think they need more communication, sex, money, etc. to have a better relationship or marriage but one of the things that truly guarantees a better relationship is gentleness. Being gentle is not a sign of weakness but an indication of strength and the love for peace.

Key of Kindness

Kindness is defined as the quality of being friendly, generous, and considerate. You may have come across the statement, survival of the fittest and Darwin's theory of evolution. Survival of the fittest is usually associated with selfishness, meaning that to survive (a basic instinct) is to look out for yourself. Science has shown that devoting resources to others, rather than having more and more for yourself brings about lasting well-being. Kindness has been tagged by researchers to be the most important predictor of satisfaction and stability in a marriage.

One sure way to be kind is to open your eyes and be active when you see people in need. Opening your eyes means noticing when others are suffering. Celebrating someone you love, giving honest compliments, telling someone how s/he is special to you, and refusing to gossip about your partner are all ideas about how to practice kindness. Kindness doesn't mean that you don't have to express anger rather how you choose to express the anger is the key. Anger is not bad but how you express it and the result of the anger is what is of importance. Practicing kindness often takes our mind to acts of generosity, like buying each other gifts. While those are great examples of generosity, kindness can also be built into the very backbone of a relationship through the way partners interact with each other with or without the gift of chocolate. My friend Irene claimed to be loved by her husband because of pecks and gift showering. Yet anytime she doesn't do what her hubby wants or expect to be done, he would immediately become furious, blaming, judgmental and even insults that goes on for days.

Irene in fear of losing her husband's love would immediately be defensive and then comply with his wishes, hoping to have control over his feelings and behaviour towards her. Irene is always afraid to do what she wanted to do. She constantly seeks permission to act on everything and monitor her actions closely in order not to make her husband angry. If you find yourself in a similar situation where you always need permission to act and the joy and passion in your relationship is stale, then kindness is blatantly non-existing in your life. Relationships thrive on kindness and love at all times. Human beings are born in relationships and our life is intrinsically fastened in the bond of relationships right from childhood to adulthood and beyond. Couples must take responsibility to practice kindness in a relationship rather than blame each other and play the card game of "I'm right you are wrong". Kindness to your spouse and yourself comes from a desire to support your good and the utmost good of your spouse and the union. You become genuinely kind when your utmost priority is to support the highest good of the relationship. But if your deepest desire is to protect yourself from getting hurt, then your first choice during conflict is most likely to be an attempt to control with blame, withdrawal, anger, compliance, resistance, or judgment. Your wife wakes up several times at night to feed and put your kid back to sleep. It will not harm to wake up and surprise her by doing the laundry or preparing food for the family. Transform to show kindness and generosity whenever the need arises. You will benefit from the application and use of this key and so will your children now and in their future.

Key of Selflessness

Love is a beautiful thing but being with someone you love and adore is even more beautiful. However, it is not always a bed of roses on a silver platter; it takes some real commitment, a lot of sacrifices, and even tears to make it work. Relationships can give you an unexpected surprise by hitting rock bottom leaving you with no other choice than to either be selfless or selfish. But being selfless is not as hard as cracking a stone with a bare hand if you truly love the person in question; it simply means accepting to love unconditionally. We all want to feel loved and adored in a relationship. However, if it feels as though you are the only one giving your best shot, you will end up feeling inadequate. A one-sided relationship is not sustaining at all. It takes two to tango, therefore two people putting a certain amount of love and effort into making a relationship work is the most selfless oxygen to a relationship.

According to a recent study, people who are motivated to care for others tend to really do well, but it is also important for you to not neglect self-care and your own needs. When love is selfish, it holds back where and when it is supposed to give freely without hindrance. Selfish partners do not feel safe in relationships because their love is conditional and they, therefore, do not support partners the way real love is supposed to. The difference in how your love is perceived by other people is determined primarily by whether it's coming from a pure and selfless person or a needy and selfish partner. Conflicts are completely inevitable in relationships because we are humans and our views and expectations can clash ones a while.

Consider those clashes as confirmation and reminder of the flow of blood in your veins carried by a mortal body. Mastering the keys and incorporating them into your daily lives will give you the experience, exposure, knowledge, and wisdom to communicate as many positive messages as possible during conflicts. Successfully married couples will attest to a common fact that, their marriage is much more functional today than when they first fell in love because they have mastered these keys over the years and their further applications and consistent usage in practice has become an integral part of their existence to the benefit of their lives collectively. It is vital to look for the good things in your spouse and communicate them through edification and building up so as to instil passion in your relationship/marriage. Relationships and marriages are subject to improvement when humility is made a foundation block of the partnership. It is healthy for couples to point out their partner's best instead of pointing out their worst. If at all the worst part of a partner has to be emphasised it should be purposes correction to the good of the relationship in a selfless and considerable manner. Humans are not immune to mistakes and therefore partners may at times be offended by the mistakes of another partner.

In the event of identifying mistakes, gentleness must be used as a foremost point of approach towards correcting the part of your partner that is disliked. Like an egg- too much pressure will break it. You need to treat each other with humility and gentleness to create a fulfilling understanding in a non-toxic environment. A thriving marriage/relationship is made up of two thriving individuals. It can only be as strong as its parts; husband and wife. The union should be seen as blending and not cloning of the two distinct personalities towards a positive end. Common sense suggests that healthy relationships emerge when healthy people come together in a healthy, positive way. This means that there's a place for appropriate self-care and self-improvement in any marital relationship. Successful couples don't consider it strange when external trials and pressures come upon them.

Instead, they prepare for hard times and make provisions to seek outside help when the need arises. In all kinds of adversity, take pains to anchor your relationship and marriage to the solid rock of the fate that brought you together in the first place. Remember, your union is not by accident but by a choice. Couples are expected to regularly celebrate their marriage with passionate sexual intimacy but sometimes we become selfish and neglect each other's feelings in the process. Sex should not be seen as a chore or obligation but as a delightful activity by which each spouse puts the other's needs and interests ahead of their own. It is wise to never lose sight of the fact that sex is not the only element of a vibrant marital relationship. Couples need to understand that satisfying physical intimacy also includes lots of affection, tenderness, warmth, and physical touch. People who require vibrant relationships need to find ways to resolve the issue of male and female roles between themselves. Talk openly about your expectations and personal preferences and come out with a plan that preserves fairness and equity in the way household tasks and responsibilities are carried out. The ultimate goal is to bear one another's burden and function as a team. Women like to naturally cook and take care of other household chores as per tradition.

It does not therefore mean that those chores become labelled as feminine and cannot be carried out by men. It is even beautiful not to officially share such responsibilities but administer them as and when one sees fit. It is selfless to discover your mate's love language and learn how to speak it. This will enable you to build each other up in some active practical ways with positive encouragement. It is an act of selflessness to nurture your spouse's strengths and supplement his or her weaknesses. Such an act requires a significant investment of time and energy, but it's an investment that pays off in a relationship capable of overcoming storms. Successful marriages are made up of two people who intentionally treasure and honour one another. This is achieved by keeping a conscious account of the things you value about each other and commemorating the blessings of your relationship in a tangible, physical way with gifts, celebrations, and meaningful moments of significant occasions. A relationship is built upon a foundation of shared value, interest, and goals. Scheduling regular date nights and outings to develop meaningful traditions and family rituals will bring a spark of romance into the household. It is also of necessity that couples learn how to maintain a healthy balance between togetherness and independence. Couples that go the distance recognize spousal conflict as inevitable and put in the effort to combat them with selfless compassionate acts. The secret of marital success lies in the way conflicts are handled. Keeping short accounts of happenings and never letting the sun go down on anger is the sure way to a healthy marital life. Those who stick together understand that marriage is a sacred and solemn mystery. Therefore, they enter into a marital relationship with the attitude that divorce is not an option. Your understanding of the fact that marriage is a lifelong adventure, filled with triumphs and defeats will motivate you to maintain and savour it at all times. But if you view relationship and marriages as a forever joy ride, you will be disappointed and end up jumping from one bust of the other in the event of challenging times. The most cherished principle of a union is to continuously press on toward the goal in both good and bad times.

Can You Spot A Good Relationship?

No one knows what goes on between any couple. Decades of scientific research into love, sex, and relationships have made clear discoveries of several behaviours that can predict when a couple is on solid ground or headed for the gutters. If you have or want a romantic relationship, then my guess is that you probably want a healthy one but what's healthy doesn't look the same for everyone. This is because people have different needs at different times. Couples' specific needs with for instance communication, sex, affection, hobbies, or values may change throughout the lifecycle of the relationship. This is why it takes maturity and something more than romance to achieve for better or worse.

A successful relationship in your 20s will in no doubt be like the relationship you want in your 30s and 40s and so forth. Nevertheless, flourishing relationships all do have the following elements well managed and active: *Open communication, Trust, Conflict Resolution, Teamwork, Physical intimacy,* etc. Making sure you understand the evolution of relationships/marriages and the challenges they come with should motivate you to master and recognise the five essential keys to safeguard your union at all its stages of evolution.

5

THE SWOT ANALYSIS OF A RELATIONSHIP

Isn't it crazy looking how relationships can be analysed with the SWOT marketing acronym? Well, I don't think it's that crazy if you ask me. To look at the dynamics of relationships from a broader perspective, SWOT analysis a viable consideration. My favourite and popular SWOT business analysis is a structured planning method used to evaluate the *Strengths, Weaknesses, Opportunities, and Threats* involved in a project or business. We can also make it useful as an exercise when trying to determine a suitable relationship. You might be surprise but by looking at your strengths, weaknesses, opportunities, and threats in a relationship you can begin to appreciate the skills that will help you to get a partner, to stay in your current relationship, and also pave way to enjoy and maintain your relationships. I am not by any means advocating the operation of marriage and partnerships as businesses, but a SWOT analysis could be a useful tool in creating awareness and positioning ourselves for long-term marriage and relationship success.

The priority for any couple should be to create goals or objectives for the relationship. Those goals are what are most important to the couple, and they should ultimately lead to a marriage of love, peace, and joy. Having a realistic perception of the current state of your relationship is highly crucial. Recognizing your internal challenges, the ones you have the most control over is good, and determining the external forces and their effect on your marriage or relationship is a great way of knowing where you are, where you are going, how to get there, and to remain sustainable in the short to long term. Both partners can be involved to take such an important exercise towards a collective good.

Many businesses use this tool when they're considering a new venture, collaboration, or goal, but it's also a great tool for marriages and for people who are looking forward to spicing things in their relationships or to even those who are in search of a life partner. The foremost step to create your SWOT analysis is to closely examine your current relationship situation and to see how your strengths and weaknesses affect it. Your end goal is to determine how you can effectively capitalize on your strengths while overcoming your perceived or real weaknesses. Thereafter, you will have to discover the potential opportunities and threats of your significant half or prospective partner.

Strengths (Internal)

When it comes to strength, you will have to make a deep visit to the core of your relationship to assess what strengths both of you have that will make a difference and make you stand out comparatively. These should be things that are within your control and that you and your spouse can build upon to make a strong union even stronger. This exercise can take off by simply making a list of words that perfectly describes you. You may also decide, as a couple, where you are strongest and recognize those strengths and seek ways to incorporate them into other areas of your marriage or partnership. Your strength could be a great way for you to cement your relationships survival and sustainability. Are you a great communicator, do you have stronger physical and mental attraction, excellent financial discipline and saving habits, etc.? Answering these questions below will help you discover specific strengths of your relationship:

- o *Which areas of your relationship are working pretty fine? (i.e. goals, communication, problem-solving, etc.)*
- o *What commonalities do you both fancy? (i.e. skills, hobbies, friends, interests)*

- *What unique differences make you "better together"?*

Weaknesses (Internal)

With weakness, you need to equally think about what areas your current/potential partner would like you to improve on. You will have to be brutally honest to yourself or seek constructive feedback from trusted and objective friends, family members, and colleagues about areas of your life that needs improvement. Partners could also jointly look at areas of their lives that are not so strong. This can be quite challenging but should honesty lead to a better conclusion because ignoring areas of your lives that need improvement will suffocate the relationship in the short or long term. The good thing about the weaknesses is that they are internal and within your control to change if honestly identified. Effective communication might be missing in your affairs and if that is the case, then you will have to recall past moments where you think your communications were not so good and rectify your mistakes going forward. Everyone has a weakness but the difficulty lies in admitting it and seeking for help.

You can discover your weaknesses with the following questions:

- *Do you bring any limitations to the relationship/marriage? (i.e health condition, financial issues, aging parents, work schedules, etc.)*
- *Do you have any specific traits of character that cause periodic fights and misunderstandings? (i.e. selfishness, harshness, passive aggression, laziness, uncleanliness, nagging, etc...).*
- *Are there any hidden agendas that need immediate attention? (i.e. an addiction, an affair, inappropriate relationships, toxic friends, etc.)*
- *Are you holding onto those indiscreet comments that confused you in the past?*
- *Are you able to put up good behaviour towards each other's parents and siblings?*
- *Will you be able to share life in your middle ages?*

Opportunities (External)

Most couples think of having a healthy marriage, better sex, and great communication, but what opportunities are you able to take advantage of that will bring you closer to those awesome goals? A lovely and responsible family and friends can be great opportunities for your relationships. You can make use of marriage ministry at your local church, or spend some good time with healthy couples around you. Anyone with positive and impactful marriage goals can be a great source to draw inspiration.

Questions to uncover opportunities may include:

- Are there people or mediums that can make us better together? (Friends, family, hobbies, church, etc.)
- Are there any other ways or resources to grow us better? (Studies, new career, business ventures, etc.)
- Do you respect each other's views?

Threats (External)

At this stage, just like businesses endeavours to look at the things that can potentially hinder your success as partners? Just as family and friends can be opportunity, most can also be a threat to the very survival of relationships. Regardless of the threats being external to the relationship, you can develop the needed power to eliminate them or at the very least minimize your exposure to them. It could be people outside your marriage or partnership such as exes, in-laws, brothers, sisters or commitments to certain specific endeavours. Your primary focus should be to ensure that the spotlight is strictly kept on the marriage or partnership. Potential threats can also be identified by carefully asking the following questions:

- Are we/ am I practicing specific behaviour that my spouse dislikes? (i.e. addiction to drugs or substances, excessive

drinking with friendships, separate pursuits, worrying spending habits, indiscriminate outings, etc.
- *Does your partner value individual ambitions to family goals?*
- *Am I engaging in toxic behaviours? (An external relationship, conversations, and company with the wrong people, pornography, drinking habits, etc.)*
- *Are we encountering circumstances that can prove difficult to the relationship? (Loss of income, Debt, health crisis, recalcitrant children, another man/woman in the picture, etc.)*
- *Do you occasionally flex economic muscles in your relationship?*

The following steps might be of enormous help to assist you with marketing yourself in a relationship:

Step 1: Determine Your Objectives

Begin to think about the next few months ahead of you and what kind of relationship you anticipate having and what kind of relationship you will be accepting in the long term say 5 years ahead if you are not already engaged. But if you are already engaged in a relationship or marriage you will have to look at what you want your union to be like and the changes you anticipate to cement a worthwhile relationship.

Step 2: Create a Strategy to Market Yourself

Have a second look at your game plan, if you don't have one develop one as a guide. Once your game plan is at play, determine which potential lovers you plan on targeting. What would your ideal partner and relationship be? How will you be finding these potential lovers? How many will you target? How long will it take? And so on. Nothing is worth achieving without a realistic plan and same applies to relationships. If you want a sustainable relationship, then a plan towards that objective is imminent. The way you present yourself will determine who you attract or how you are treated in a relationship.

Step 3: Develop a Strategic Plan of Action

Break your marketing strategy into different parts and plan out each section respectively. Include what you will be doing and when it will be done. Give yourself ample time and make sure you prioritize the actions on your strategy in order of importance. The knowledge you gain from analysing your relationship or marriage will help you to gain a clearer understanding of your relationship structure and it will allow you to take a strategic step towards its survival and benefits to both partners. The end of the year is a great opportunity for you to pause and reflect on the year coming to an end and to look forward to the year ahead. With this book being a perfect end-of-year gift, try to schedule some time with your partner to do some analysis of your relationship. The following areas might help you in the process:

- *Regular Time Together*
- *Finances*
- *Parenting*
- *Communication*
- *Holidays and Celebrations*
- *Extended Family Relationships*
- *Health*
- *Sex*
- *Spiritual Growth and Development*
- *Recreation*

You can do this by stating your answers separately and converging together for discussions or better still do it together. This important exercise will help you to learn from each other's perspectives, voice your opinion on how things are going, and devise means to overcome areas identified as threats. It is never easy to have enough time, place, or the right opportunity to discuss relationship issues but this SWOT analysis provides a good opportunity to talk about things you might probably be ignoring or do not know how to go about. You may in certain instances, ask yourself what others see as your strengths, weaknesses, opportunities, and threats. The stringent focus should not be placed on what others think but if there is a consistent gap between observer's perception and what you consider reality, then take that as a red flag and pause for re-evaluation. Be mindful whilst following this analysis because some of the things can be pretty hard to talk about. Keep an open and civil mind and follow the effective rules for arguing whilst at it. Remember that you love each other and what you are doing is to strengthen your bond to pave way for happier future endeavours. Relationships like any other entities come with strengths, weaknesses, opportunities, and threats.

If for whatever reason you think your relationship doesn't have any threats then you are either being dishonest to yourself or missing something that might haunt you badly sooner than later. Consider relationship or marriage as a commodity with a limited shelf life. You are an asset to your spouse, and your spouse is an asset to your life too. In the past, marriage was a long-term investment "till death do us apart" but lately, it has been reduced to a pathetic short-term investment by some people. Hopefully, it does not reduce further to a trader's investment. Most modern-day relationships/marriages are neither an asset nor a liability to each other. People simply live a neutral life without emotions and real enthusiasm.

6

TOXIC FRIENDSHIPS TO A RELATIONSHIP & MARRIAGE

Friends play a crucial role in our lives, even after marriage. You must engage in good friendships that do not only benefit you but also impact positively in your relationships. Toxic friends are like bombs waiting to explode. You have to understand and be able to identify the character of friends, whom could be hazardous to your relationship or marriage, and decisively handle them before it becomes too late. The "bad company corrupts good moral quote" is for all Christians but it is equally applicable to even non-Christians because its meaning deeply reflects the real effect of hanging around toxic people. It is easy to go with the flow and do what everyone else is doing, even when you know it is wrong, simply because everyone is doing it. I'm not saying you shouldn't have friends with different believes, rather be smart with the situations you found yourself in with them. The following will serve as indicators that will require your vigorous attention:

A Friend Who Bad-Mouths His/ Her Partner and Others

Growing up, my parents were very strict with us regarding the friends we hang out with and the families we visit. I remember them banning us from playing with certain specific individuals in the community or going to some particular houses to play. We were never happy with those restrictions because the houses and people we are banned from, were the very people and places we wanted. It took time to heed to those restrictions after realising we had no other means than to comply. It was during the later years of our lives when we could interpret things correctly that we realised how well they meant.

Their reasons and cautions had always rested on the fact that; we will become exactly the people we hang out with as in the adage "show me your friend and I will tell you your character". It's amazing how easily we can take up the behaviour of the people we keep as friends and be influenced without noticing it. If your friend consistently talks negatively about his/her partner, then over time you will naturally start to see your partner unfavourably. As friends, you will like to validate or make your friend feel better when he/she begin to slice a partner into pieces. To make your friends feel better after telling you all the nasty stuff about their partners, you indirectly validate and allow those thoughts to gain root in your mind. With time, it becomes normal to also practice what you have learned from your friend's ill-act and eventually end up hurting your relationship or marriage. To have a good relationship and marriage, it is necessary to surround yourself with friends who are not overly negative about their own partners.

A Friend Who Talks Negatively Of Your Partner

Some friends easily jump to say everything negative about your partner at the least provocation with a disguised intention of protecting you. Beware of such friends because they usually validate their negative tendencies by the fact that, they may probably have known you long before you got into a relationship with your partner. When you allow your friends to say whatever nasty thing they want to say about your partner, you are indirectly putting your friendship ahead of your relationship or marriage. Friends who consistently bash your partner breeds negativity into your mind and heart. This leads to the formation of toxic co-dependent friendships that will eventually collapse your relationship or marriage. You may have noticed that some friends only thrive during conversations that involve frustrations or obstacles that you and your spouse are probably experiencing. Others do not receive positive news about your partner too well. They display a lukewarm attitude and have a way of chipping-in a comment to discredit the positive news.

Such friends are ironically very vocal and critical whenever you talk about differences between you and your partner. It can be extremely frustrating for you to deal with the negative things you hear from those friends when you are particularly going through a hard time yourself. Try as much as possible not to allow such calibre of friends to stigmatise your relationship or marriage as negative.

Close Friends of the Opposite Sex

Friendships with people of the opposite sex should be carefully evaluated because of the likely risks associated with such friendship. Friendship with someone who was a former lover should be avoided by all sense and purpose. Any friend whom you feel might make romantic advances on you should also be avoided at all costs if you don't want to invite poison into your relationship and marriage. The evolution of marriage clarifies that being friends with a person is not the same as being in a relationship and equally not the same as being married. Friends' understanding of certain issues from your relationship or marriage might be far different from reality. Such friends may sound as helping and much understanding but their contribution in most cases go to soothe our hearts in the short term but not enough to solve the problem. Be sure that your spouse is your number one friend and significant person.

A Friend Who Hates Marriage

It is not likely to have friends who share 100% of your likes but friends who hate marriage while you are married or seriously considering marriage are not worth your time. There may be friends whose perspective on certain aspects of life differs from what you perceive. It is simply beautiful and normal to have friends with different opinions and perceptions of certain aspects of life but those with hatred and bitterness towards marriages for whatever reason needs to be tamed.

An all-negative friend who does not want anything to do with relationship or marriage and its associated commitment will serve no good purpose to your relationship as a friend.

Friends with Different Moral Values and Ethics

Surrounding yourself with people who do not share the same or similar values and ethics will be difficult to keep as friends. They will be unable to provide you with positive dynamics to support your relationship and marriage. For instance, if you are a Christian, your friends should be able to respect that fact of your life whether they are of the Christian faith or not. Hanging out with people of different ethical values will only make way for a personality clash that will bring toxicity to your friendship and impact negatively on your relationship or marriage with a partner. In today's world of diverse integration and religion, it is possible to have friends and partners of other religious believe but an open minded person will understand the dynamics for a mutual relationship. If you want to keep friends with different values then it should be those that are flexible enough to accommodate each other's differences.

Liars

Some friends thrive and only gain recognition and power by telling lies that make other people miserable. Such people are crafty in what they do such that, they can convince you beyond any reasonable doubt to believe in what they say as the truth when it is in-fact a blatant lie. Subjecting yourself to these lies regularly will in no time affect you and your relationship. Once you have identified your friend as a liar, it is important to distance yourself from them to avoid being an influence to a level of destruction. Remember this; chances make our parents but choices make our friends. You have a choice to choose and change your friends at any time. Don't feel bad about cutting ties with a friend who proves to be toxic by their quest to embrace lies and dishonesty.

The following are typical biblical examples of people who were corrupted by toxic companies:

King Ahab's pagan wife corrupted him to do more evil: The marriage of King Ahab to Jezebel is a true reminder of how bad association can corrupt good people. The wicked queen, Jezebel, in the quest to remove the worship of God from Israel, killed many prophets of God. King Ahab was in the know of her wickedness, yet he gave her his seal of approval.

Solomon's pagan wives corrupted him: King Solomon was the one that offered a thousand plus sacrifices to God in Gihon, and was the same person who supposedly requested wisdom at the hands of God and said a heartfelt prayer during the dedication of the temple in Jerusalem. Solomon was the same person God appointed in David's stead to build Him a temple. God was said to have appeared twice to this same Solomon. The question then is, could there be anything that would turn such a person's heart away from God? The answer turns out to be, yes! Something did change him; and that which changed him was not false teachings, nor persecution but rather, his contact with evil women. He had seven hundred wives of royal birth and three hundred concubines, and his wives led him astray. King Solomon, later in his life, was described as one who did evil in the sight of the Lord and it was ungodly women who led him there. Indeed, evil communication corrupts good manners.

Amnon's friend Jonadab corrupted him to do evil: Absalom, David's son, had a beautiful sister called Tamar from another mother, who was a virgin. David's firstborn was so obsessed with her that he fell sick because of her. Jonadab was a crafty friend of Amnon's. He convinced Amnon to tell him his problem as he could see Amnon was not feeling too well. And Amnon told him that he is in love with Tamar but did not know how to get her. Jonadab immediately advised him to lie down on his bed and pretend to be ill. He also did tell him that when his father comes to see him, he should say that he wants the sister Tamar to come and give him bread and prepare food for him to eat. Amnon took Jonadab's bad advice, lay down and pretended to be sick. And when King David, his father, came to see him, Amnon pleaded with the king to let his sister Tamar come and make some food for him to eat. Amnon made sure that everyone in the room was gone, leaving him and Tamar. Then Amnon asked Tamar to bring the food closer for him to eat. But when she drew closer to Amnon to feed him, he seized her and demanded that she have sex with him. She refused and pleaded with him but Amnon would not listen to her, and being stronger than her, he forced himself on her and raped her. And afterward, Amnon sacked Tamar from his house. This act Amnon was deceived to do, cost him his life two years later. Absolom, the brother of Amnon, avenged his sister by killing Amnon. The saying is therefore true that evil communication corrupts good manners.

King Jehoram of Israel was corrupted by his wife, Athaliah: One other sad story of how a potentially good person fell and perished due to the influence of bad people is the case of King Jehoram, the son of King Jehoshaphat. By and large, it was the influence of an evil wife that turned his story into a tragedy. Indeed, evil communication corrupts good manners. Evil communication from toxic friends should be avoided at all cost to prevent it from impacting negatively on your relationship.

"The righteous choose their friends carefully, but the way of the wicked leads them astray."

Proverbs 12:26

7

MEANT TO BE OR NOT MEANT TO BE

The beginning of a love life is always nice pleasant. For some reason you see everything you expect to see from the other partner. When things get a bit tense in the relationship, the same person who endorsed the idea of *"meant to be,"* takes a quick flip to "we are not meant to be," how ironic. People with strong destiny beliefs think that their partners are either meant or not meant to be. They see conflict in relationships or marital difficulties as indicators that they are simply not compatible with each other. Those with strong growth beliefs on the other hand believe that they can cultivate a quality relationship by working and growing together. The strong growth believers view difficulties as opportunities to develop a stronger relationship. Your marriage or relationship is not a fulfilment of an ancient prophecy. It is ultimately your utmost mandate to endorse it with ideas that will elevate it to its romantic level. Whether a relationship is meant to be or not, depends largely on the amount of effort that is sacrificed into it. You will agree that true and stable love is not built on simply thinking that someone is attractive and compatible on the surface and that just because someone is not like you, or even that you are direct opposite, does not necessarily mean you aren't well-suited to be life partners.

Green-light for Commitment to a Relationship

To be committed to a person towards a sustaining relationship, one must identify certain elements in the person before making that life choice. The following serves as a green pass before that big life-changing decision:

Supportive partner: it's magically refreshing to have a partner that supports your hope and dreams. A man who believes in you and pushes you to go after your dream is divine. Men with low self-esteem, in particular, become insecure for instance at the progress of a partner's career. They sometimes feel disappointed with themselves and therefore kick against any effort to transform your life, instead of supporting you to a greater height.

Listening ear: Every person deserves listening ears and so does your partner. We've all had thoughts and fears that are hard to share at certain stages of our lives. Nonetheless, it's important to put your emotions on the table to increase the bond between you and your partner. A good partner will make you feel safe when you share your thoughts, not embarrassed. You feel better after talking to them, not worse. You equally show them respect and enormous support when their emotion is on the table too. A good listener can listen to someone without taking what they say personally no matter how difficult the subject matter may be.

No competition: The two of you are not in competition against each other to determine who is best in whatever you both do. You want the other person to succeed in whatever they do because you realize that their success doesn't make yours any less. You both help each other grow into the best versions of yourselves. A partner whose attitude and behaviour revolves around an effort to outperform you cannot in any way support your growth and life improvement.

Prevalence of similar future needs: If you've been in the relationship for a while, you surely may have had an open conversation about the future. You may have discussed kids, marriage, career plans, and your finances. You trust each other enough to know that no matter what happens, you can have a future together that will make both of you happy. In that case, you can be sure of no big surprises such as your partner wanting a bigger family while you only expect one or two.

No fighting: Like really, who wants to spend their lives fighting? Certainly not me, and I doubt you want it too. Fighting with your partner can only build tension and create unhappiness. Having a constructive disagreement is a productive learning tool. If you can steer clear of fighting whenever you disagree with an opinion, then you are on the path to a great relationship. A partner who resorts to fights and other forms of abuse will in no doubt do the same when in a commitment.

Family love: Families can be very tough and tricky to deal with so if you have a partner who is tolerant and loving to your family, then you are on the right path with the right person. Partners who have regular issues with their own families will find it difficult to develop a love for other external families. It is great to have a partner who is approved by your siblings and equally approves your family and siblings.

Your connection is beyond superficial: You are not only with this person for their job, status, financial means, looks, or an idea of them, and vice versa. Superficial relationships have a short lifespan and a bad ending.

Good intentions: A partner without the diabolical intention of using you and the relationship for personal gains has good intentions for the union. You will in the face of a potentially good partnership if you both put in the effort to help each other in the journey towards a common goal. You consider each other equal in the relationship and don't take each other for granted. Some people will support anything you do even if your actions are wrong and dangerous to yourself. Such people are selfish without any good intention and will walk away the day you encounter problems that will need their undivided support.

Don't hold your past against you: Partners who can get over your past and move forward with you in the relationship are gems. You both accept the past for what it was: a learning experience. They trust that if you made mistakes in previous relationships, you're not going to make them again with them.

If they also have a not so "clean" past, you accept it and trust that they are not going to hurt you. Remember, everyone deserves a second chance.

Discuss sensitive subjects without qualms: You can convey your bedroom feelings to your partner without them thinking you're dissatisfied with your intimate life. If they are uncomfortable about an aspect of your relationship, you're open to hearing about it too.

Honesty: Surely, you had fun with friends when you were young but as you grow up, you look out for someone you can depend on not someone engrossed in games that will lead to hurtful feelings and arguments. You talk to each other about insecurities rather than storming out and blowing off steam with friends, leaving your partner at home to worry about what you are doing or not doing. People who intentionally try to make you jealous just to feel cared for are a wreck to relationships.

Respect your independence: While it's great to spend all your time with your better half, it's important that each partner has enough alone time and is also able to maintain their relationships with their friends and family. You take space if you need it and your partner equally does so without feeling neglected. You both take pride in your independence in trust and faithfulness. After all, if you can't survive in your alone time, how can you function together.

Your values are in synchrony: In addition, to being head over heels in love with each other your views in life, moral values, beliefs, and style should fit together to some extent.

Recognise the importance of the person: he/she is your greatest teacher and the one who challenges you, drives you crazy, stirs and ignites your deepest passions.

A friend sent me a message saying: *Richard, I love my boyfriend but he doesn't do anything for our relationship. I don't remember the last time we went out, or he did something romantic.*

He is usually out with friends drinking. We've been together for five years, but he won't propose. And yet he doesn't want to break up. I'm looking at getting married. I thought we were meant together but I am thinking otherwise.

This is quite strange but very likely and happening. There are honestly quite a number of people in that same or similar situation. They are unable to understand that, they cannot date a woman for more than one year without considering further commitment towards marriage. You have no business asking a man whether he wants to marry you or not. The signs will be all over for you to see from day one. Does this friend sound like you? If that is the case, ask yourself whether you can identify the signs above in your relationship. If not then you have some real work to do. Whether you are meant to be or not isn't the contention here. This is because there should be something special about this man that made you cling to him for five years. Look inward and find out whether you are exhibiting the traits of a woman to be relied on for marriage.

In most cases, women decide to remain in a dead-end relationship because of some material benefits they fear losing or the fear of not getting another man or worse of all falling into the same situation with a different person. Such fear and assumptions will make you risk staying in a lifeless relationship for far too long and by the time you consider leaving; you might have invested too much time, material, and emotion. Low self-esteem men will threaten to cause harm to you if you consider a breakup due to their investment into you and the relationship. The longer you stay in a stale relationship the more toxic the relationship becomes and the more danger you create for your life. Many women have been murdered as a result of leaving a lifeless relationship that time and emotions have been invested into. If you cannot determine if a man will marry you after a year or more of dating, you have to withdraw before it becomes too late to do so, unless you are not interested in marriage.

But if you are not interested in marriage, then what the hell is your business with a man for all this years who has no intention to add value to your life in an official commitment. A colloquial Afrikaans word "Vat en sit" meaning to take a partner to settle down without formalities that comes with marriage is what most people settle for in the long term. But if you can vat en sit what is the fear of marriage as a formal alternative? The challenge that comes with cohabitation is that there is a risk that you partner can evict you at any time without a second thought and you cannot claim a spousal maintenance from him. You will invest your energy and emotions to build a relationship and probably amount wealth and property for which you cannot claim ownership of unless you are nominated as a beneficiary at the demise of a partner.

"The only person you are destined to be with is the person you accept wholeheartedly and equally accepts you wholeheartedly in synergy without any hidden selfish motives."

Richard Ofei

8

UNDERSTANDING YOUR PARTNER'S PERSPECTIVE

Your overall perspective of the relationship is seriously affected by your limiting beliefs, needs and developed rules that influence your expectations from the partnership. A person from a place of mistrust and insecurity will surely take a distrustful perspective to their relationships. You will end up with a consistent assumption that your partner is cheating or doing something untoward or better still doesn't love you as he/she promises to. The opposite is true too, if your perspective is rich in self-love and confidence, you will be in a consistent position of creating a supportive and trusting relationship. It is no doubt that we are unique entities with diverse strengths and weaknesses. We therefore go into relationships with different perspectives to our lives that are influenced by our past experiences, both personal and those that we witness from other people. This is where emotional intelligence becomes an important aspect of our lives.

Your ability to change your perspective in relationships is a key aspect of emotional intelligence that equips you with the ability to empathize and connect with others. Your emotional intelligence will lead you to the understanding that, no perspective is more valid than the other. Emotional intelligence is your ability to identify, evaluate and manage your emotions as well as the emotions of others. It is common knowledge that the smartest people are necessarily not the most successful or the most fulfilled in life or relationships. It is of no surprise to come across academically brilliant individuals having real struggles in their relationships and other aspects of life. Your intelligence quotient (IQ) isn't enough on its own to achieve success in life or relationship. Your IQ can undoubtedly help you get into college, but it's your EQ that will help you manage the stress and emotions when facing your final exams. In the same vein, your intelligence and smartness can get you into a relationship but it will take your EQ to be successful. Both are highly effective when they work in synchrony to build-off one another. Seeing and accommodating another point of view doesn't always come naturally. It requires an effort, and the following strategies will assist you to see your partner's perspective in a relationship.

Make your relationship a priority: Remember, life is all about choices, and choices are powers embedded in humans that cannot be taken away by any other human or supernatural powers. Not even God can interfere with the choices we make because they are free wills granted to us Him. You can resolve conflict amicably by choosing to put your relationship first or otherwise. It's imperative to put your relationship first by making effort to understand your partner's perspective. This will bridge the divide between you and your partner as unique individuals with different views of the world around you. Doing so will strengthen the connection between you and introduce a juicy dynamic of trust, where your partner feels that they will be accepted and understood no matter how far their feelings or beliefs deviate from your definition of reality.

A healthy relationship is not an easy journey but seeing things from others' perspectives will help you become more conscious in your relationship. Your partner will effortlessly feel more loved and secure for an enviable time together. There may be situations where you will find it difficult to see things from your partner's point of view even if you give it your all. But when such a crunching time arises, focus on the bigger picture and set your ego aside, and do away with anger and fear to invite love and security. Don't forget that the most challenging times can bring growth if well managed by making the relationship a priority.

Desist from using unproductive bad habits as your weapon: Ignoring and denial are one of many weapons used by people when there is an action or a form of disagreement that requires correction. When couples disagree, some of them take up the weapon of denial subconsciously. They do this by out-rightly refusing to believe what the other person says or insist on a certain narrative as defence to feed their ego.

Be a listener: We live in a smaller world where relationships are of no respect to the cultural background or language of a partner. You and your partner might even speak the same language but will have different meanings and interpretations associated with different words and phrases. This is primarily due to growing up in a different environment with different experiences. Exercising good listening skills can help overcome communication barriers that will create understanding at a greater level. In the course of a relationship, partners directly or indirectly demonstrate different thoughts and feelings that are of importance to them. The problem however is that most people only absorb just a fraction of what is communicated. To grow in understanding, you have to condition yourself to listen to understand and not listen to respond.

Depersonalize your partner's behaviour: Make it a point to see your partner's behaviour more objectively. This will allow you to discern the underlying need instead of reacting to just behaviours, and it will enable you to respond instead of reacting. The next time your partner is stressed and it feels like he/she is taking it out on you, take it easy and don't personalise his actions before developing in-depth understanding.

Be courageous and ask for clarification: A lot can be misconstrued and misunderstood when tempers are high and it does no good to relationships. Courage to seek clarification in the most modest way is a sure recipe for understanding to break the barrier of confusion. Phrases such as, "I'm not sure I understand", "Can you please explain to me?", or "I don't think I'm getting what you mean are golden "statements carrying an underlying message that the relationship is important and that "one wants to understand" rather than worsening situations by saying "you are the problem" or "I don't want to know". My friends, Dineo and Nkosi have been married for 5 years. When Dineo is away from Nkosi, she thinks of how much his partner doesn't help out around the house enough or she dwells on recent misunderstandings and fights they engaged in. Joe has been in a relationship with Naledi for 5 years too. When he is away from Naledi most of the time, he thinks fondly about past moments or major positive memories.

The crucial difference between the two relationships is how positively or negatively they view their partner. Dineo is allowing negative sentiments to override her judgement, while Joe dwells much on a positive sentiment of his partner and the relationship. This is a clear indication that their overarching view of their partners, and ultimately their relationships, is seen through either a positive or negative lens. Developing a positive perspective of your partner and your relationship leads to effective problem solving during conflict and makes you to generally see your partner in a more positive light, even at stressful and difficult times. Being engulfed with negative sentiments or negative perspectives, on the other hand greatly distort your view of your partner to the point where positive or neutral experiences are perceived as negative. People who dwell on negativities do not give each other the benefit of the doubt in relationships.

Tony Robbins discusses the power of empathy and gives people three questions to consider in ensuring that they're considering their partner's perspective: "What are you seeing that I am not? What have you experienced in your past that has led you to this belief? How can I use this as an opportunity to know you better?" The media and television programs that perpetuate the myth of combining romantic love with a happy-ever-after ending have done women a great and dangerous disservice when it comes to relationship. Women are somehow conditioned to crave that big love of ecstatic lifestyle.

It's painful to note that a lot grew up idealising marriage with romance as the best part, but if people will have a more realistic understanding of its cold, hard benefits, things would have been done differently. A lot more walked away from relationships that might have made them happy because of their misunderstanding of the fact that what makes for a good marriage isn't necessarily what makes for a good romantic relationship.

Is Your Partner Not Listening?

Successful relationships are all about healthy communication and listening to each other effectively. However, it's easy for partners to experience moments where talking to each other becomes a challenge and listening becomes virtually absent. Lack of listening in a relationship can be a sign for bigger problems yet to blow up in the faces. Oftentimes, it's easy to blame a spouse for a particular problem but faulty communication is a two-way affair and both could be guilty. Lack of listening or the absence of attentive listening could emanate from either wrong way of delivering information or personal problems or better still a combination of the two.

Whichever of them relates to your situation, it's worth being truthful to yourself, your partner, and the situation itself by approaching the issue of contention without hurting each other in the process. In the case of the way you say things, remember and keep in mind that the way you say things is as important as what you say to others. A beautiful and potentially fruitful conversation can be sabotaged by a reckless negative and argumentative tone of voice coupled with aggressiveness that is devoid of respect and consideration.

If you are serious about having your partner as a good listener for the sake of a peaceful relationship, consider the following and their accompanying solutions:

Ulterior Motives: The Macmillan dictionary says "if you have an ulterior motive for doing something, you do it partly because you think you will get some advantage from doing it. You have to be straightforward and not attempt to take advantage of situations otherwise your partner will with time sense a pattern of manipulation in your tone of voice and decide to ignore you. Try to avoid being manipulative and passively aggressive at all times; otherwise, your partner may think you are on a mission to take advantage of him or her even if your actions are not intentional.

"Honesty is the first chapter in the book of wisdom."

Thomas Jefferson

Flirting with old Baggage at every opportunity: Old baggage is previous knowledge and experience that a person may use or be influenced by in new circumstances. This happens anytime conversations about topics or issues that have already been discussed at length previously is brought up again to attempt to tune out a partner. If ever you have lingering issues that need to be dealt with or something that requires forgiveness, have a decent conversation about it and put it to rest. Bringing out old issues to justify a certain stand will only lead to further communication shutdown and unimaginable problems.

"I've been alive a long time, long enough to know that the more baggage you carry in life, the more unstable you'll be, until eventually, you get sick of carrying it, and then you just fall down".

Rebecca McNutt

Reactive conversations: To be reactive means reacting to events or situations rather than acting first to change or prevent something from happening. History of overly reactive conversation in a relationship can lead to the partner not listening or being listened to. A partner who doesn't listen may be using it as a coping mechanism to avoid overly reaction from the other partner. If you find yourself always reacting in defence of yourself at the least provocation, take a deep breath and think about what you want to say. Try to identify alternative meanings to what you want to responds to from your partner before jumping to negative conclusions that might further complicate your moments. The objective of having conversations as partners is to develop understanding to support each other in the process. It should never be seen as a marathon of words that require a winner.

"The language of reactive people absolves them of responsibility."

Stephen R. Covey

Unnecessary Negativity: Negativity is an attitude in which someone considers only the bad qualities of a situation or person and not the good ones. If your partner complains that you are always negative, you may feel justified or think that it's their way of deflecting attention on their negativity. Whichever way you look at it, consider your tone and the way you address issues at stake. Even if you're "right," there is always a way of handling issues more positively or neutrally to avoid problems. Focusing on the negatives at all times can cause others to ignore you. Make it a point to focus on solutions rather than dwelling on problems. Desist from constantly making comments full of accusations.

"There are some people who always seem angry and continuously look for conflict. Walk away; the battle they are fighting isn't with you, it is with themselves."

Unknown

Your partner could also be ignoring you for reasons that do not concern you in any way. They might not be listening to you due to a fault of their own and wouldn't listen to you regardless of how well you communicate with them. Such reasons could include but not limited to:

- *Your partner may be distracted by something not related to you that is making it hard for them to give you their full attention.*
- *Your partner might not be interested in the subject at stake*
- *They may disagree with you and do not want to hear your advice or opinion*
- *They may be avoiding an attempt to hurt you by staying mute or avoiding you*
- *Your partner may also feel intimidated by your sense of reasoning and will rather avoid giving you a listening ear*

Relationships are meant to bring us happiness but unfortunately, not everyone enjoys it. If your relationship is fraught with listening problems, then look inward and figure out what you want and correct all unhealthy tendencies that need to be corrected, so as to position yourself towards a fulfilling change.

9

THINKING ABOUT YOUR EX

"My hubby has been getting on my nerves over the past few weeks, and all I could think of was how my ex would have acted differently," said Naledi. Sounds familiar right? Some people can't get over their past after a break-up. They have an unfinished emotional-attachment issues. They harbour feelings of guilt, anger, regret, and pain. If this speaks of you, then you have to heal before jumping into any new relationship boat. It's normal to miss your ex, especially if the breakup wasn't orchestrated by you. According to Laurel House, a dating and breakup coach, you're not ready to be in another relationship until you don't think about your ex for at least one day and feel comfortable being alone. But just because you're thinking about your ex doesn't mean you're meant to be together, and that he/she qualifies as a comparative element to your current or future partner.

There are reasons why past romances keep finding their way into your head, but none of them have to do with remained feelings as some claim. You could be stuck, thinking about your ex because you liked him/her, but if so then this has nothing to do with that person but everything to do with you, which is the more reason why you have to let him/her go off your thoughts. You can always be that person again, whether it's with a new person or on your own. The way you feel about your experience is only natural to anyone who has shared emotion and intimacy with another over a prolonged period of time. The thing is, such thoughts don't come to mind because you necessarily miss your ex, but because you probably didn't anticipate a breakup and it was not initiated by you too. If you initiated the breakup and still feel that way, then it's high time you focus on the unbearable situation that led to the break-up. Did you probably over-react or acted on impulse without a thorough understanding of the situation before your decision to calling it quits? Well many fall victim of such situations but the good news is that you can always forgive yourself and reconsider your decision if only your ditched partner still has a place accept you back. If you don't intend to go back, then there is no point in wailing rather stay positive and find something engaging to focus on instead of occupying your mind with an ex you left on your own dereliction.

I have heard people say, "he/she is the only person I have ever been in love with so it's not easy" not to think of him. But that doesn't mean he/she's your soul mate either. It just means that you are capable of love and that you'll find love with someone else and unleash this feeling again, but you have to close the door on your ex for good first. Social media seems to be both a blessing and a curse in instances of breakup if one is an active user. It can allow you to keep in touch with as many people as you like on your own time. It's also a great way to get support and make connections but it tempts people to take a look at the profiles of their ex to see what they are up to, and that is one of the mistakes. A breakaway from social media to avoid seeing things from an ex that will irritate or guilt-trick you is quite a good decision until you developed the strength to move on.

Thinking about sad thoughts from the past constantly is the same thing as a dog going back to his own puke. "As a dog returns to his vomit, so a fool repeats his folly." What you need to do is to constantly tell yourself that you are not a dog and that you wouldn't keep returning to your vomit. I perfectly do conform to the fact that, time heals all wounds but who has the time to wait while getting bad grades, being emotionally drained, falling behind at work, losing friends, and perhaps suffering an unexpected heart attack or other health crises due to substance addiction as a result of an ex? One effective action against struggles with unresolved feelings following the end of a relationship is to think back and consider the bad sides as well as the good. What influences most people to get stuck in the past is cherry-picking and only dwelling on the isolated incidence of good times spent, but no relationship is perfect. If it was all that perfect and rosary you wouldn't break up in the first place. Recognising the flip side of the relationship and what lead to the breakup in the first place can be an important part of understanding why things ended. The end of a relationship can sometimes be an opportunity to do some of the things that you didn't have time to do before, like concentrating on your hobbies or seeing people you haven't seen in a while or take up a study just to redirect your focus and attention for a new or improved career.

Finding a healthy relationship partner is a rare treasure without a specific time frame. So it's best to pick up yourself at the earliest possible time after a breakup to avoid reeling in pain far more than necessary. The earlier you heal, the better your chances of readiness to either accommodate a potential partner or redirect focus on your single life towards work, career, or something worthwhile. You need to be well prepared to avoid questioning a good relationship that might come your way after a break-up. It is acceptable in some isolated circumstances to think and be tempted to text your ex. This statement must be carefully considered as one's situation needs to meet certain specific conditions for the action to make sense and impact positively. It is particularly possible when there are greater signs that you two might be able to reconcile and put the past behind. There are surely instances where partners can truly reconcile after a break-up and reunite stronger than ever. Such signs include the ability to express and demonstrate genuine accountability and remorse for having hurt another. Anyone can change for a moment, but being flexible and sustaining real change can only be exhibited by a real gem of a life partner.

The key to reaching out to an ex is to expect absolutely nothing because expectations can lead to let-downs and further disappointment. It's imperative to note that, texting your ex and thinking about them is a no-go area when you are already in a relationship after a breakup or your ex has also moved on. Some people entertain a certain fantasy that the reconciliation of romance with an ex can lead to some good love. Such fantasies must be killed deep within as soon as one of you moves on. Being informed of an ex's new relationship is a guarantee to move on with your life. Painful as it may feel, it will be a golden gift to you. You must be able to differentiate between neediness and the impulse to return to a negative relationship and the hope for an improved relationship with your ex. This can be achieved through self-awareness and honesty in your situation to avoid developing a desire to be in a relationship simply because it is familiar or fears of being alone. If you are thinking of rekindling an old flame, then you are not the only one but you will have to reconsider it through the following:

Leopards' don't change their spots: This age-old saying means a lot and relates to what we often see in relationships. A situation where a person may not be willing or able to change his/her character means that his/her bad habits have no chances of renewal. This can be a real set-up for the heartbreak that will likely lead you down the same path again.

Toxic relationships: Toxic relationships before break-ups have chances of resurfacing upon return if there is no rehabilitation from bad habits. If you can loosen yourself from the grips of an abusive partner, whether physical, emotional, or both, then you should count yourself lucky and not become part of statistics.

The side chick situation: If you left the relationship as the other woman, a return is sure to cause you more emotional pain and suffering. A return sends a wrong indication that, you don't know your worth and cannot live without your partner and that you love him/her more than yourself.

Selfish partner: Some people are only loyal to their need for you and once that need is satisfied, you are nothing but just one of the lots. Chances are you will be discarded as soon as he is through with you again and again.

Unresolved your issues: If issues that led to the break-up are not well resolved, there will surely be a repeat and continuation of the problematic relationship. A second chance will inherit additional issues that will not get better resolution leading to a ripple effect of past problems. The time spent thinking of your ex-partner after a breakup can be attributed to the way your brain processes loss and rejection. Remember, traumatic events such as unwanted or unexpected breakups can cause intense psychological distress that may lead to physiological discomfort. When you prioritize your partner more than yourself, your self-worth will automatically be based on them. This external source of self-worth in the person of your partner makes you feel loved and cared for, but as soon as the relationship ends, your self-worth comes crashing down, and it becomes harder to build yourself up thereafter.

It is therefore crucial to always maintain your hobbies, friends, and activities separate from your partner for a healthy relationship balance. People who have trouble thinking about their ex are usually the ones who were broken up with, as opposed to the ones who initiated the breaking up. The initiator of the breakup or divorce usually comes to terms with the fact that he/she no longer wants the partnership and therefore can psychologically move on without a second thought. Although there's no single, simple solution in black and white and situations may differ, reflecting on this piece will help you gain perspective and – with time – begin to accept what's happened for the sake of your future relationship endeavours. Stop giving your ex "free rent" in your mind so that you can move on with your life positively.

10

KINDLING ROMANCE TO IGNITE SPARK

Braaing on a weekend, holiday, or special occasion is a South African tradition. I have grown to love and appreciate over the years. There's nothing more South African than a braai, the country's version barbeque enjoyed by family and friends. The cultivation of the fire using wood or charcoal is a true form of art and is usually carried out by the host or the braai-master. If you have ever set fire for a braai, you know that you have to use kindling. The smallest spark can eventually become a roaring fire. Once the fire has reached its full potential, you have one of two things to do; maintain it to stay strong or neglect it to die out. The same strategy can be adopted by a relationship. Whether your relationship is new or old you need some emotional rekindling to add passion into it to maintain its relevance and spark.

Most of us get so busy with other aspects of life and wake up one day to realise that, we don't feel very close to our spouses anymore. The painful truth is that it happens to the best of us all. Life has a way of making us starve our relationships and marriages through jobs, in-laws, church activities, kids, travels, misunderstandings conflicts, etc. Couples become less sexually active as their relationship matures due to life demands and the presence of kids who needs to be taken care of. Kindling romance and instilling spark in a relationship does not always mean sex as we often assume. A simple genuine act of character towards a partner can ignite a relationship to a happy end.

Ignition Keys

Make yourself attractive: if you make yourself more attractive, your spouse will often become more attractive to you. Ignoring your outlook and appearance will over time make your spouse negative. Negative changes in your appearance can precipitate negative responses from your partner in the same way a positive appearance will attract positive reactions.

Spicy tips

Nothing beats attractiveness more than taking care of oneself daily as a partner. Personal hygiene, grooming, and good appearance are a sure way to make yourself attractive and irresistible to your partner at all times. Stay attractive and be on top of your kindling relationship goals.

Hold hands: this might be seen as trivial but it is skin-to-skin contact and therefore promotes intimacy. According to science, when we touch someone, our body releases oxytocin, a chemical that produces happiness and comfort. So, the more contact you have, the more oxytocin you produce. Oxytocin strengthens empathy and communication between partners and it's proven to be a contributing factor for long-lasting, happy relationships. Holding hands with your partner will improve your relationship and create a bond that will impact the quality of your relationship significantly.

Spicy tips:

o Walk side-by-side with your hands brushing against each other, but not holding
o Hold hands lightly with a flimsy grip
o Clasp your hands with fully interlaced fingers
o Touch his/her face with one hand, while the other hand holds your hand.

Break from tradition: habits and rituals are somehow comforting but it's sometimes necessary to break from tradition and surprise your partner with something new. If your partner always does the laundry, take the initiative to do it on one weekend. You will be surprised at how your partner will feel and react to that simple gesture.

Spicy tips:

Take a break sometimes: Allow yourself to try something new that could lead to establishing another tradition of choice. The traditional way of doing things in a relationship becomes a financial burden over time or a time constraint which causes more anxiety than fun and leads to boredom. Do something new that breaks your routine as a couple. Whatever you do, try to find one thing that makes the day feel a bit more different by altering your daily routine positively. Skip home food and try a new restaurant. Don't go to your favourite restaurant that you have frequented over the years, try a new dish from a completely different outlet.

Think before talking: the environment of trust created to establish the union between couples is too precious to be damaged by a careless comment. Reckless name-calling and related personal attacks are mood killers and will negatively impact your relationship. Remember that insults and nasty name-calling take just a few seconds to rattle off but can stay longer in a relationship. Compliments often dwindle after being with a person for a while. You end up taking your partner for granted and unconsciously believing that they will always be there. It is vital to wake up from your slumber and self-deceit to spice the relationship with compliments before it's too late. A genuinely honest comment that does not look like randomly praising what does not even require praise is a thoughtful action worth emphasising. Compliments become meaningful when you focus on specific things that are truly unique to the individual.

Give your spouse a compliment: human beings thrive on praise and positive feedback and distinctly want to do whatever it takes to get more of it. Therefore, if you want more good things make sure you acknowledge them. Don't forget to make a point of telling your partner when they look nice or when that food she cooked tastes so delicious.

Spicy tips:

- Thank your partner for loving you the way they do; "Thank you for loving me the way you do, you bring the best out of me".
- Let her know you appreciate his/her love and efforts; "you are the pillar of this family".
- Send your partner words of affirmation; "I'm glad to have found you, I will always love you".
- Let your partner know that you are not taking them for a ride especially in situations where there is something in particular they always attend to for the good of the family; " I appreciate the time you spend with the kids away from your busy schedules", " thanks for the outfit".
- Give a sexy compliment to boost your partner's confidence; "you are charming and tempting me to sin".
- Compliment your partner for their parenting roles; "you make the best husband and a special dad to our kids".
- Compliment him/her on the way they treat you; "I appreciate your support whenever I needed them." I know that as long as you are around I'm safe". "You are my pillar of strength".

Laugh together: One effective way to add positive interactions to your relationship is to laugh together. Look for ways to often laugh together because laughter sets a light-hearted tone in a relationship making couples feel safe. There is a general belief that the rate and manner at which you and your partner laugh together indicates the strength of your union. You may sometimes provoke each other to laugh and that clearly can increase relationship satisfaction. It is not healthy to ridicule each other because that can harm the relationship. However, finding humour in little provocation that can spark laughter is a fabulous trick to bond even better. People have different tastes in humour, so be sure to know what amuses your partner in order not to sound offensive or negative.

Spicy tips:

- Don't be afraid to be silly with the weird things your partner finds hilarious.
- Observe her while watching TV and identify what makes her laugh and make comment on it to spark even more laughter.
- Talk about a real-life story and laugh at your own mistakes and bad lucks.
- Learn to embellish the little moments in your life when you for instance get a mild electric shock from fiddling with an electrical appliance.
- Limit your TV moments and shows that you both enjoy and make you laugh at.

Doing something you suck at will invariably bring laughter because there is often no pressure to succeed at it and you do not in any way take yourselves seriously in those instances. Something you know that you will fail at accomplishing will surely force laughter to brighten the home. Try being awkward and weird sometimes, you don't always have to be on your best behaviour in a relationship. It's fun to just intermittently do things that are not typical of you.

Check your body language: It's not what you say but how you say it that plays a role in the effect it brings to the relationships. To avoid misunderstanding, couples should aim at an awareness of how they carry themselves during discussions. Before you open your mouth to speak, your body has spoken. The greatest bone of contention with relationships is that it's your body language that throws everything off the cliff. You may sometimes practice what to say to an attractive lady or guy upon meeting, but all that won't matter if your body language portrays insecurities contrary to your confidence. If you want to come across as confident, attractive, and friendly, you have to unleash the right physical signals.

Spicy tips:

Flirt without a single word at selected times that will not feel awkward. Men and women undoubtedly send some of the same body language signals at all times because they are both a product of the human species. Notable flirty signals including but not limited to fussing with hair or clothing, glances or prolonged eye contact, little touches, casually fidgeting with your hair and clothes will indeed send a good signal. Indulge yourself into your partner without talking or saying much. Your body and that of your partner should be in synchrony with your action rather than words. If this is carried out in the right manner you will become more of who you are while attracting the right people and experiences to yourself. Try declaring who you are and what you want to be through posture. People are unfortunately subconsciously judged by their posture in appearance. Portraying a positive posture will invariably give a positive perception of who you are. It doesn't matter whether you are old or young; making sacrificial changes can drastically change your future social situations and even change how you perceive yourself.

Leave the past to the past: healthy couples invariably live in the present and work hard towards a better future instead of dwelling on past mistakes and problems. Consistent concentration and reference to the past create unnecessary resentment that keeps partners from moving forward. It is good to learn from your mistakes but equally important to keep your past out of current issues to allow the continued growth and progress of the relationship. You must understand that it will be highly impossible to change the past, but you can work toward a better future by committing to focus on what you can change, rather than what has already happened.

Spicy tips:

Learn to forgive yourself and others at all times. You can never move on progressively if you do not honestly learn to let go, forgive yourself and others, forgive situations and leave the past in the past. Regardless of your past mistakes, you can always work on a better future with perseverance. Every person has had some sort of a painful experience in life at some point but how we react to those past experiences determines whether we can gaze into a successful future life or not. Be determined to jump out of your comfort zone into completely different terrain. Taking steps away from your comfort zone comes with some level of discomfort, but being able to master the courage to move forward could bring you an everlasting reward. This process is a work in progress and not an immediate decision with an instant result. Regular outward baby steps in precision will lead to significant progress over time. If the first step does not work, keep trying other ones until you are completely satisfied. In that way, you will be able to discover a lot about yourself that you probably never gave a thought to. Elevate yourself past your fears and the result will amaze you in the end.

Stay positive and speak to yourself with encouragement refraining from negativity to progress positively. The notion of all men being cheats and all women being slut is a myth that should never be entertained in your wildest assumptions. Just because your last relationship had such elements or your friend went through similar cheating relationships does not mean your future is destined to be the same. Be positive and affirm that; your previous relationship or your friend problems are no what define you and your future relationship prospects. And that you are going to work to love yourself and your partner regardless. Positivity breeds positives and negativity breeds negatives. Stop victimising yourself and blaming others at the least chance. You need to take responsibility for your happiness, and not put such powers in the hands of other people, especially those that hurt you. It is a choice to either feel bad about another person's action or to begin feeling good about yourself in all situations. Playing victim feels good on the inside but the painful reality is that no one cares. You may not easily forget another person's bad behaviour towards you or a certain situation, but you can ultimately forgive and move on. Forgiveness shouldn't be seen as a sign of weakness but as a tangible way of empathising with others and looking at things from their point of view, for the sake of a peaceful progressive life. Don't live a life defined by pain because it can only hurt you more and invite unnecessary stress that will negatively impact every aspect of your relationship. I strongly believe that what you do with what or who hurts you is quite important than the associated pain.

Do not habitually paint people that come into your life with the same brush. Do not for once bring past wounds into a new relationship, thinking all men/women are the same. It serves no purpose in painting your new partner with that old brush. The mere fact that you couldn't trust your previous partner does not necessarily mean you cannot trust others. It's absurd to assume that your new partner will leave, just because your previous one left. Make it a point to be in control of your expectations. We have all been let down by people or situations for some reason or the other in our lifetime; it's not the best of feelings. But this is large because we place unrealistic faith and expectations in people and situations, and get hurt if the outcomes do not meet our desires. There are no guarantees in this life of uncertainties. Move on and be in control of your expectations when things do not go your way or when a situation or a person overwhelms your innate expectations.

Look for the soft emotion: A concept thought by psychology states that; behind every "hard" emotion is a soft one'. Behind the mask of anger is an emotion of sadness or disappointment. Trying to figure out the vulnerable emotions underneath your partner's hard display of anger will help keep you connected as a couple because you will be better equipped to empathize with their true emotion.

Add elements of surprises: Surprises mimic the emotional state of a new romance and little gestures go quite a long way. Adding elements of surprise can rekindle the relationship to maintain a spark. If your relationship is on the rock, find a way to redirect it to bloom. We often lose relationships as a result of anger which could have been controlled. Agitation and hostile response usually lead to disastrous relationships. Being lovingly kind can guarantee you a good relationship because good people are always loved by their partners.

Nobody rejects a loving partner who always cares and respects them.

"*It is better to lock up your heart with a merciless padlock than to fall in love with someone who doesn't know what they meant to you.*"

Michael Bassey Johnson

11

The Concept of Age in the Choice of a Partner

The conviction of seeing oneself when the time comes to consider whom you get attached to in a relationship or marriage, can make or break the choices you make. The issue of age is a typical concern to most men and women alike regarding the prospects and possibility of a long-term relationship. I have been asked this question on countless occasions; what is the right age to get married? What should be the ideal age gap between partners? The right age for marriage is the age of maturity and readiness of the individuals' concern. A person may be older and yet lack maturity and readiness for the commitment and responsibility that comes in marriage. Many people have missed the opportunity to have a lasting and prosperous marriage and relationship with acquaintances as a result of the conviction that one partner is older or younger. The only person too young for marriage is the adolescent who is still under parental care and the immature or premature adult who still needs to grow up in maturity.

There are pros and cons to marrying a younger person as well as an older person. Again, what is vitally important with regards to age is the state of mind of the person in question, the maturity level of the person, level of commitment to a union, ability to respect and understand the purpose of relationship or marriage, and its accompanying factors. The choice of a partner's age in a relationship largely rests on the short and long-term future needs of the couples in comparison to their current state. It is a biological fact that young people have greater chances of conceiving as a result of their high fertility rate than their older counterparts. A man without a child, considering settling down with a woman will therefore ideally opt for a younger matured lady with a high propensity of conceiving and the ability to raise kids and shoulder the responsibilities of a mother. It is however necessary to open your age range filter to include all reasonable ages. In so doing, you will increase your chance to end up with a whole group of folks to date and a greater possibility of finding a significant half. Tapping into a larger pool allows you to find love and a perfect match. Biology depicts that younger people have much more sexual energy and stamina than older ones. However, having someone who raises the bar and encourages you to bring the best in your sex life and romance to the table can be heavenly. Being open to the idea of a younger female is a wise decision to be taken especially by a man who is trying to grow or start a family. This is true because it is biologically easier for younger women to fall pregnant and carry a child than older ones. Women who are interested in dating younger men will also be fortunate to have men who may be open to using surrogates if both partners agree to that route.

Overall, regardless of the age difference, all relationships are the same. If your relationship is based on love, trust, and good communication coupled with other key ingredients of a successful relationship and marriage; you and your partner will be as happy as any other couple on earth. There are no formulas, rules, or equations regarding the age of partners in marriage or relationships except the natural route of wisely and diligently following your heart in truth and honesty. It is important to have an eagle look at the life stage a person is in to determine if your values relate to each other's. Successfully significant relationships are purely based on mutual understanding, connection, and compatibility rather than chronological age. The success of a relationship depends largely on the extent to which partners share values, beliefs, and goals about their relationship.

It also depends on the support they receive from each other in achieving personal goals, the fostering of commitment, trust, and intimacy, and how they by and large resolve conflicts in synergy. All these factors unfortunately have little or absolutely nothing to do with age but maturity and level headedness. It is a common belief that women place much importance on the status and resources of their male partners because they are child bearers and the investment in rearing a child is high on their side in terms of time and effort. They are therefore comfortable with partners who can also invest resources into the relationship. This is not in any way related to those who see men as mine site for exploitation. Men in contrast value attractiveness more than women because youth is seen as an indicator of fertility from the point of view of evolution. Because men cannot bear children, they are naturally attracted to younger women to enhance their chances of bearing kids of their own. This does not also mean that men should exploit young women to satisfy their libido. With more working-class women in the equally good position of companies, earning equally good wages and salaries like men, most women do not rely on men for resources like the old norm. The reality and truth are that, while the age gap may come with its challenges as any other thing, age should by no means be a barrier to a relationship.

The society holds a negative stigma regarding age difference and it, therefore, makes people have a feeling of doing something wrong when they develop feelings of love for a person not in their age bracket. Before shutting the door on the possibility of finding love, think about the level of maturity of the person you are considering and your ambitions for the future.

Your potential partner might be older than you but it doesn't mean he understands his position in life more than you. If both of you share similar values and want the same thing from the relationship, then you are ultimately midway to have a wonderful partner. On the contrary, things will be difficult if you both want different things. Maturity develops after a lifetime of experiences and the ability to handle relationship to satisfaction is an individual affair. No one wakes up and becomes mature as a result of his/her age. Experience happens to people at different times in life and therefore causes some to grow faster or slower than others.

Signs of Maturity

We are all impressed by people who carry themselves well and show signs of maturity. The list below will give you an indication as to whether the person you are anticipating as a will-be partner is intellectually, emotionally and spiritually mature:

- *Ability to keep long term commitment*
- *Not destabilise by flattery and criticism*
- *Not consumed by drawing attention to themselves*
- *Knows how to set priorities*
- *Thinks (seek wisdom) before acting*
- *They make decisions based on character and not feelings*
- *Feel more empathy and concern for others*
- *Mentally prepared to face challenges*
- *Tolerate feelings of discomfort and finds a solution to it*
- *They are optimistic*
- *They do not take everything personally*
- *Take responsibility for their health and happiness*
- *They respect other people's opinion*
- *They are encouraging and supporting*
- *Stand up for justice for themselves and others*
- *They do not cling to material items or bragging*
- *They find joy in other people's success*

Some of these indicators will expose what you are lacking in your journey towards discovering a significant half but let it be a lamp to brighten your path through discovering and accepting a significant partner. Irrespective of your position in life, whether as a couple or a person on the path to discovering a better half, remember we are all imperfect but noticing and acknowledging your shortfall will pave the way for you to work towards bridging the gap towards personal growth.

People with emotional maturity realises that a relationship is not one person imposing their will on the other. Each relationship is different because the personalities within the relationships are different and an adaptation is therefore of great importance.

"Love is not about finding the right person, but creating a right relationship. It's not about how much love you have in the beginning but how much love you build till the end."

Anonymous

12

RECIPE TO A HEALTHY RELATIONSHIP & MARRIAGE

A functional "GPS" on achieving a sustainable relationship is a sure recipe to a positive life. The path to a happy marriage is far from easy as today's divorce statistics depict that many couples may not complete the journey. This will lead to the build-up of resentment in the hearts of several people. It is much easier to blame failed relationships and marriages on not spending quality time together, lack of communication, and allowing bitterness. These aspects are in no doubt important recipes for nurturing a happy relationship or marriage. Their absence is a sign of a much deeper problem and until this deeper problem is holistically addressed, no seminars, books, and any amount of external modification can bring meaningful changes to your relationship. To get clarity on what these deeper problems might be, let's visit the holy book for divine insight:

"One of them, an expert in the law, tested Jesus with this question, "Teacher, which is the greatest commandment in the law?

Jesus replied, "Love the Lord your God with all your heart and with all your mind." *(This is the first and greatest commandment)*

[Love your neighbour as you love yourself] *(This is the second greatest commandment)*

This biblical extract is so powerful that it can be borrowed and planted into our marital relationships as a major ingredient of our recipe for awesomeness.

I strongly believe that all relationship and marital problems can be traced back to one or both partners failing to adhere to these two biblical principal laws. [The golden rule in this instance is that the minute we begin to focus on our wants and needs over those of our partner; we are destined for deadly tsunamis hitting us from all angles of life.]

The Effective Recipe Follows:

Never go to bed angry with one another: Being angry over hurts and grievances can be dangerous to any relationship or marriage unless it is addressed in a timely and mature manner. After all, no one is perfect and both partners are of the same team so being gracious enough in admitting to a short-fall or mistake is a simple win-win scenario.

Be clean, decent, and orderly: disorderliness, laziness, and untidiness can breed disrespect and ultimately affect affection for one another. Modest and well-groomed personalities are important for both partners. It is the responsibility of both partners to create a home environment that is clean and orderly. Most women neglect to carry themselves attractive after marriage and indirectly frustrate their men into losing interest in them.

Keep God in the centre of the home: Unless the Lord builds the house, they labour in vain who build it. A Godly home can stand the test of time with a greater chance of being successful. Godliness can give us the mandate to overcome bitterness and disappointment of any kind to restore love and happiness.

Keep your family problems private: Private family matters should never be shared with others outside your home-not even parents unless critically and absolutely necessary. Be truthful to each other at all times without deadly secret closets. Avoid telling jokes at the expense of your partner's feelings and strongly defend each other whenever the need arises.

Criticism and nagging: Critiquing, nagging, and finding fault in your partner is a sure way to destroy your union. Expecting perfection will breed bitterness in you and your spouse, so try by all means to overlook fault and hunt for the good things in your spouse. The secret of a successful relationship or marriage is not in having the right partner but in being the right partner.

Respect your privacy: all humans have a God-given right to personal privacy. Infringing on each other's privacy unnecessarily is an antidote for destruction. Tampering with each other's messages, emails, purses, and wallets without permission is a sign of disrespect and mistrust. Spend less time trying to curiously figure out what your spouse is up to and rather find ways and means to please him/her. Marriage partners do not own each other and should therefore not push too hard for personality changes.

Always be your authentic self: Some people put on masks and different personalities depending on who they are with and the situations they find themselves in. Refrain from being a chameleon to be accepted or loved by your partner. Be your authentic self and let the development of love take its natural course.

Agree to disagree: a successful relationship or marriage is not without disagreement. Successful and loving couples respect the point of view of one another and use humour over their points of contention to avoid unnecessary tension. Agreeing to disagree is a sign of maturity and love.

Determine and identify your partner's love language: Each individual has a unique way of communicating or feeling loved. Preferences and hobbies are not universal to gender. Couples must observe each other and identify the little but important ways in which their partners show love. Love language doesn't get the needed attention in relationships but it is one of the secrets to a happy relationship.

For some it could be, picking kids up from school, washing cars, keeping the home tidy, ironing, preparing a particular meal, etc.

Never take your partner for granted: it is human nature that, once we get comfortable with what is familiar, we unconsciously or consciously slip into a state of complacency. Avoid complacency at all costs and offer respect to your partner at all times.

Never use Divorce as a threat: Do not threaten to break away to get your way out of a situation. Making threats to a partner is not a mature and fruitful strategy to solve marital or relationship problems. Constant use of languages such as Divorce and separation at the least provocation is bad for the growth of the relationship. Those who often use such languages usually do so as a controlling mechanism and must therefore be avoided at all costs.

Sex and faithfulness: do not put anything in your mind or in front of your eyes that could compromise your faithfulness. Guard your sexuality daily and devote it solely to your partner. It is imperative to note that, whenever we offer moments of our emotional intimacy to another person we indirectly sacrifice sexual faithfulness to our spouse because sexual faithfulness in marriage goes far beyond just our bodies. It also includes but is not limited to our eyes, minds, hearts, and soul.

Honesty and trust: the foundation of any healthy relationship or marriage is in its honesty and trust. Trust does not happen; it takes time to be registered in two or more people. You can easily understand, be committed, and be selfless towards a certain goal in a moment, you can show patience with less effort and time but to build or re-build trust takes time and something extra to accomplish. Criticism and defensiveness are a serious threat to trust in any relationship or marriage. Couples who stay together in trust know how to fight without being hostile to each other. Trust makes couples respond quickly to each other's needs and easily makeup after a fight to repair their relationship.

Give thanks and appreciation: when one partner feels gratitude, both partners will automatically become more satisfied with the relationship. People tend to experience gratitude on days when their partner does something thoughtful. In the long run, those who experience elevated levels of gratitude also experience stronger relationship commitment and are less likely to break up. We can perhaps find time while we are bathing, gardening and cooking to think about ways in which our spouse has invested in our marriage or relationship. Doing this will not only boost our gratitude and relationship commitment but also increase our overall happiness.

Do away with the grass is greener where you water it myth: To have a successful marriage and relationship it is vital to resist this myth at all cost, that is someone else will make me happy. You need to learn to put your energies into making yourselves and your marriages better. No one will make you better than you can make yourself.

See love as a verb and not just a feeling: Everyday life wears away the "feel good" side of relationships and marriage with time. Feelings and happiness will fluctuate but real love is based on a couple's vow of commitment "for better for worse" – when it feels good and when the feeling is not so good. Love should always be a work in progress and not something static.

Do you see yourself in the ingredients outlined? Are you falling on the negative or the positive or better still somewhere in-between?

Whatever your answer is, take a deep breath and embrace yourself for a change that none other than you can effect to gain through this nutritional fact as you proceed to read further:

- *100% balance life*
- *100% happiness*
- *100%fufillment*
- *100% understanding*
- *100% respect*

All served with *Love, Peace & Care*. There may be some variations regarding the quantity of each ingredient at specific times of our lives but if all exist at all times then we are well-positioned for success. Anytime you feel like you are unable to let go of something your partner did; just add a pinch of Trust. When you are frustrated about life and it's affecting your relationship; blend kindness and patience together for your meal. When you are disappointed by your partner's actions and inactions; add a cube of compassion and considerable compromise to taste. When you deviate from your relationship goals at some point and you are in doubt; stir-fry all ingredients with Love. Remember, loving another person is a matter of choice. If you are in a relationship, I hope you chose to love your significant half with an honest heart and open mind, and willingness to compromise and understand each other.

Sex is simply a dessert ingredient in a relationship. Imagine sex as part of the ingredients for the main course meal of a relationship, I think that will be awful. Dessert just kind of finishes off after everything is rightly positioned. My take on the desert is that it is all good and compliments the relationship in a wonderful way. Relationships that are built dominantly on sex lack the pillars to long-term survival. It is easier to have sex than to have a relationship. I sometimes have problems with the way most people define sex in a relationship. I prefer the definition to be expanded beyond penetration. A relationship that sees sex as ingredients for its main meal only sees sex as an act instead of looking at it as an ingredient for intimacy building and connection. Contemporary society's standards around sex are highly impoverished that, most people are only able and interested in talking about how much sex they are having. The proliferation of paranoia in most instances shifts the real purpose of sex. Relationships are bound to go through different phases of life. People get ill at some point in time, others feel stressed out by life events, and all will at some point experience aging too. All these circumstances can shift the amount of sex desired by partners and will cause serious frictions in relationships that are solely dependent on sex.

The idea that sex gets stale in a long-term relationship is a diabolical myth. It gets much better over time if it is well understood and defined the right way. Some people mistakenly organise their sex life around what their partner wants instead of what they want and need. You should be able to also take the initiative to invent what inspires your needs when dessert is on the table. Sometimes, you can ask for a fruit platter instead of the usual ice cream or yoghurt.

The strongest relationships often have the following tools for mixing and preparing all the ingredients outlined as recipes here:

- o Emotional and psychological compatibility tool: A blending tool for developing a deep understanding of each other.
- o Social compatibility tool: The state of partners enjoying and fancying similar or the same things in life is a sharper tool.
- o Sexual compatibility tool: A mixing tool that combines all other ingredients for mutual bonding and connection.

"Compromising your beliefs for the sake of gains is lack of integrity but compromising your beliefs for the sake of greater understanding with your spouse is called wisdom."

Fawn Weaver

13

MR RIGHT & MRS PERFECT

When we were teenagers, we usually dreamt of finding our very own Prince and Princess at school and parties. The problem with looking for the perfect mate is that there's no such thing as the perfect mate, it's an illusion. The idea of finding the perfect soul mate makes men and women think that there is one perfect person out there for everyone; a certain magical force will unveil them at an appointed time. There is no soul mate because there is nothing like a perfect person for anyone on this planet. In high school, all the guys set their eyes on that one beautiful girl whereas the girls have their attention fixed on the hot guys. As we grow older and mature, our priorities for a guy or lady changes and we start looking for something greater than looks, such as emotional and mental compatibility.

Finding the Mr Right and Mrs Perfect often seems impossible and non-existent. Many people have a checklist for the adventure of securing the right or perfect partner. Good men and women seem to be few and very far between, and when we find them they are ironically and painfully taken. Single women often expect the right guy to simply walk into their life and sweep them off their feet. I'm not saying a woman should just give herself away for men anyhow but the idea of seating down and waiting effortless sounds a bit awkward. If you by any chance want to wait, then wait in principle by actively preparing yourself for your future spouse through focusing on making sure that you heal from all past and present negative tendencies and set standards that are worth keeping. This will undoubtedly prepare you to easily identify and be identified. Whilst waiting for God's time and intervention as it's always assumed, make it a point to continue learning, growing, and honouring your life with compassion during the waiting period.

Relationships are dynamic and they continue to change as indicated in the evolution of a relationship. They change to reflect circumstances, stresses, and the everyday ups and downs experienced by both partners. How you respond to relationship changes is vital to its survival. Once you are hooked up, a great point worth considering is the evaluation of your contributions to the relationship. Ask yourself, are your actions directly or indirectly impacting negatively or positively on the happiness of your partner? It is imperative to note that, your actions do not occur in isolation as they have a direct influence on both your partner and your shared relationship. One of the main reasons we attribute to not being married or remaining single is the fact that we profess not to have found the right person. In this age of online dating, many people are caught up with looking for their "perfect match", forgetting that sometimes opposites attract well to complement each other too. A successful marriage is less of the right personality and more of the right practices.

Every marriage, irrespective of a person being with the right partner or not requires much effort for sustainability. A successful marriage/relationship is built upon an unwavering loyalty to each other in a committed covenant. People's personalities change, but commitment never changes. A study published in Mass Communication and Society found that, if married women believed in the television portrayals of relationships, they tend to be less committed to their pairings and finds alternative partners more attractive. Our televisions are flooded with movies and soapies competing for viewership on a daily basis. Most of these programs portray a perfect relationship to viewers and we are often tempted to relate and compare what we see in those series to our relationships. The relationship between you and your spouse is not a movie but a reality. Excessive exposure to television makes some of us tend to question our commitment and that of others in a relationship. With the recent proliferation of social media and dating apps, our social circles have broadened and made searching for the perfect match both easier and more difficult through levelling the playing field.

But what exactly is a perfect match? You want to find someone you can talk to openly, have fun with, and share pertinent interests and activities with. Compatible with each other breeds understanding, equality, and respect. You don't have to spend every waking moment together with a compatible partner to feel secure or comfortable in the relationship. Love may be encountered in different forms, and romantic love, on the one hand, is often characterized by intensity, engagement, and sexual interest. But while romantic infatuation can cause a rush of feel-good chemicals in your brain to make you feel he/she is the one, it may not last a lifetime.

Studies have shown that a woman's satisfaction in a relationship depends on emotional aspects, whereas for men, physical aspects of sexual intimacy are more important. It is clear therefore that, men and women are attracted to different things as common compatibilities in partners. But similarities in attitudes, personality traits, behaviours, and beliefs can strengthen the duration of a marriage or relationship to a fulfilling end.

Then again, how do you know he/she is a match? There is no one-size-fits-all answer to this question because people have varying levels of compatibility with different people, and relationships on the other hand require pretty much hard work. Some may be lucky at the early stages, whereas others may struggle for years before coming across someone they want to settle down with. Instead of looking for Mr Right or Mrs Perfect; you should try to be the right or perfect partner because the only person you can truly change is yourself. Therefore, for you to meet the ideal partner, you have to become your ideal partner first and foremost. At the end of the day, your perfect partner may not be the perfect person to whom you are dreaming; rather, it will be someone who is comparable to you and is ready to invest in creating realistic harmony with you towards the future.

How to Be a Better Partner

It is important not to enter into a relationship to be made happy by your partner. You will be highly disappointed if your happiness depends on someone else. You can however learn several skills and develop yourself while in the relationship. Note that, each partner is responsible for the health of his/her relationship. The beauty of love is that, if you truly love your partner you will want to be the best person you can be for them. The good thing about being a better partner for your found prince or princess is that you can do it to enrich yourself as well as your love life. Here are some of the best ways to make yourself the person your lover deserves to die for.

Don't be afraid to admit wrongdoing and to render an apology: Don't be afraid to say you're sorry. Saying you are sorry isn't a sign of failure or weakness but refusing to admit it is.

Listen to understand and not to reply: In this fast-paced life, the tendency to listen to merely have a reply has become common to most people. We therefore fail to understand each other because we are too quick to respond.

Encourage your partner: Focus on the bigger picture to encourage and support your partner to grow and become a better version of him/her. It's impossible to grow and become a better person in an unhealthy relationship. If you're someone who is verbally, physically, or sexually abusive, ask yourself if this behaviour is helping you and your partner to grow.

Desist from repeating mistakes from the past: Reflect on what did not work well in the past and think of ways to approach situations differently going forward.

Be less selfish: The time you share shouldn't always be about you. Show genuine interest in how your partner's life is going and whether they are getting closer to the achievement of their life goals.

Value your difference: most often than not, we value the things we have in common with our partners than our differences. Relationships will be incredibly boring if partners become photocopies of each other. It is lively and rewarding to found common grounds in the things you both value and also celebrate your unique differences.

Be Happy, Not Right: Just because you don't agree with your partner's opinion on a subject doesn't mean that he or she is wrong. It simply means they have a different perspective on the subject. You can be a better partner just by trying to understand and validate your partner's point of view and feelings.

"Once you are committed to yourself, others will find it worthwhile committing to you. Nothing beats falling for a person with a good self-esteem."

Richard Ofei.

14

ARE YOU WITH MR RIGHT OR MR RIGHT NOW?

Your quest to meet Mr Right must be cautiously cultivated to avoid the possibility of rather meeting a Mr Right Now. For argument's sake, Mr Right is that one person who is deemed compatible enough to be considered as a partner. Mr Right Now on the other hand is that other person who is always ready and available to hang out with. Mr Right now most often comes disguised as Mr Right and people fall for them woefully. Use these red flags to readily spot a Mr Right Now:

Mr Right Now's physical attraction outweighs their long-term emotional bond.

Mr Right Now dodges topics concerning commitment. "I enjoy spending time with you; let's just enjoy what we have now".

Mr Right Now will fail to recall details about you, and the things that matter to you because his/her focus is time-bound.

Mr Right Now's comments and praise revolves around your attractiveness because he/she is not available for a long-term partnership.

Being acquainted with the difference between these two "Rights" is a sure path to choosing who will complement your quest for a sustainable and sound relationship.

Mr Now is always ready to party till dawn and do things you wish you wouldn't remember in the morning.

Note the Difference

Mr Right makes you happy whereas Mr Right Now never makes you unhappy. You look at some people and you immediately can't help but romance with the idea of how you got incredibly lucky to be with them. But Mr Right Now wouldn't have the same effect on you. It's not that he makes you upset but you're just sort of, whatever about him/her.

With Mr Right Now, the relationship very much revolves around sex, drinking, or fun. But with Mr Right, sex will be great but your relationship would still carry on without sex because there's more to it than just that.

Mr Right challenges you to be a better version of yourself; Mr Right Now doesn't see the potential and just goes with the flow.

You're sometimes going to fight with Mr Right because he sees how far you could go and want to push you beyond your limit, and call the spade a spade. With Mr Right Now, it's not that he doesn't believe in you but he cannot challenge you enough. He takes you the way you are and doesn't give a damn to necessary changes or growth in you. You usually fall for such people and like them because it's just nice to have someone who embraces you for who you are and lets you be comfortable in your skin. The reality is that we all grow and will need a person that will help us in the process of growth to be an awesome version of ourselves.

Mr Right often comes along when you least expected it whereas Mr Right Now is very timely. Your relationship with Mr Right just sort of happened out of the ordinary through some memorable situation. Mr Right Now comes through forcefully for lack of a better word.

Irrespective of whatever chemistry you could relate to, Mr Right Now is often chosen for a reason other than because you simply liked him and want to be with him. They mostly show up in your life when you are bored, trying to get over an ex, or all at a time when you just want to fit

in because your circle of friends is either married or engaged. People also give in to such people because they probably happen to be the first to express love towards you when you most needed it.

Mr Right will be there for you whereas Mr Right Now expects you to take care of him/her and you can't necessarily rely on them. We currently live in an era where the age-old mantra of giving away women for marriage at a tender age irrespective of their level of independence has finally been replaced by encouragement to postpone that milestone in pursuit of high ideals like educational career and true love. Many woman in this age no matter how successful and ambitious or how financially and emotionally secured they feel panic occasionally coupled with desperation when they hit the golden age of 30 and still unmarried.

I'm pretty much sure that, there is single 30-year-old or more women reading this right now who may be saying that I have no idea what I'm talking about. Well, there could be a certain insignificant number who might not be bothered but the truth is that a greater percentage of the female population will relate to what I am saying here. I will challenge many to take a good look in the mirror and try to convince themselves they are not in one way or the other worried being single at the golden age of 30. A good look in the mirror will bring you to terms with an in-depth reality of your feelings through the mirror of your soul that you're being disingenuous to think you are not worried.

When you are chasing deep romantic love, there is the fantasy that a certain level of passionate intensity can make you happier. Settling down with Mr Right in the context of your descriptions might be a viable option, especially if you're looking for a stable and reliable life companion than being lured by Mr Right Now. People often confuse Mr Right Now with Mr Right. This is so because most people go on rampage scouting for someone without being able to differentiate between who is considered right and right now. In the process, they have an encounter someone they click with and think they have hit the jackpot.

And because they want it to be true so badly out of desperation, they get carried away without carefully evaluating their compatibility. Things only become clearer after spending some quality time around each other with level-headedness. No one in their right senses should settle for a relationship that lacks respect, commitment, consistency, and dedication. A journey into what you are currently experiencing in your relationship will determine if you are in a relationship for the right reasons as partners or acting as a servant to a master or making yourself a master over a servant. There is, quite frankly, nothing in Scripture that says you have a duty to marry or be in a relationship with a particular individual. Whether we marry, and who we marry, are spoken of in Scripture as part of God's "permissive will," something He allows us to choose. We ought to own up to our choices and take responsibility for our actions in the choice of whom we marry or chose to be in a relationship with. Since we will have no one to blame for our choices, it behoves on us to make a careful decision when it comes to marital issues.

15

ATTRACTION MAGNETS OF A UNION

It should come as no surprise that physical attractiveness is recognized as an emotional need for many people, especially men. That is what drives the booming of the beauty, diet, and plastic surgery industry of our present generation. It is therefore absurd to note however that the desire to be attractive becomes superficial as soon as people are united with a partner as couples. I am often quizzed as to why many no longer care about how they present themselves to their life partners after committing to a relationship. Some level of relaxation in your own home is naturally expected and normal, but it is not a route to ignore efforts at taking care of yourself.

It is very difficult to be honest with your partner by telling them that you no longer find them attractive. That is considered a hurtful statement and it can damage the ego and dismantle the overall confidence of a partner. A little effort to buy them a new outfit, invite them to the gym, or something that could bring a change can go a long way to help. The burning question however is what if those little efforts do not work? What if they do not take you seriously and are not ready to embrace change? You will be left with no other choice than be direct and hurt their feelings or not saying anything at all leading to further frustration. As frustration goes unchecked, one eventually looks for ways to avoid being intimate with his/her partner and the relationship begins to unrealistically suffer from a chronic romantic defect syndrome. It's not uncommon for the passion, sexual tension, and romantic energy in a relationship and marriage to naturally dwindle.

A sense of familiarity with each other begins to show itself as the relationship, but there are lots of couples with highly charged intimate relationships after decades of marriage. Such neglect can build up little, unprocessed arguments and resentment quietly in your partnership. Like anything worth having, getting the spark back will require a bit of effort. The following **KEYS** will help you become magnetised in the relationship to bring your best self to the union. Remember that many of the following keys are not things that you'll be adopting 24/7 but a consistent effort in practice will work heavenly with time.

Lighten Up

When a man does something wrong, the usual reaction of a woman is to get upset and angry but this is a huge turnoff to men. Men are not so smart and not so fast, hence it is important to not be overly serious with them at all times. Taking a light-hearted approach may let a woman get her message across better to her man and at the same time remain attractive to him.

Keep a Youthful Attitude

Men are always attracted to the inner youthfulness of women. However, youthfulness refers to "child-likeness," and not "childishness." Despite the many obligations and responsibilities that come to life especially with relationships, choose to always be willing to participate, curious, and excited about things. Be child-like at times but don't ever be childish.

Practice Good Hygiene.

It is no brainer to note that simply practicing good personal hygiene such as bathing regularly, brushing your teeth, shaving, etc., makes you look fresh and inviting. No one wants to cuddle up a dead body or someone who smells and appears shabby.

No Lashing out Your Frustration

Most people accumulate all the negative emotions they have experienced throughout the day or week and lash out at their partner when they do the slightest thing to annoy them. "Never treat your spouse or partner as a trash bin". Men should be considerate and lenient when the need to make complaints about something that is purportedly the fault of their partner arises. Lashing out at the least provocation will grow to become a negative norm and a cancerous impediment to happiness and mutual respect.

Honour Reasonable Requests from Your Partner

Small gestures that cost you little can have big payoffs in how your partner feels about you and the relationship. Put on that nice cologne or hairstyle your spouse finds attractive.

Have an Attractive Body Language

Communication is said to be 55 percent body language, 38 percent vocal tone, and seven percent actual words. That is why women who talk and behave like men are never attracted to men. Men find smiling women very attractive and surveys have shown that men like a woman's smile more than her figure. It does not mean that you have to be in a party spirit all the time. A little mystery in women is a sweet bait to lure men to an ecstatic irresistible island of no return. It is a huge turn-off to act like a man's best friend after knowing him for just five minutes.

Be a Loving Partner

Having both healthy self-esteem and self-respect contributes to your attractiveness as well. Remember though that loving someone begins with loving yourself. You can't claim to love your partner and neglect yourself.

Compliment Him/ Her

While most men aren't predominantly driven by praise, they still very much appreciate a genuine compliment from their lover once in a while. Don't just say things because you think he/she wants to hear them.

Make Your Happiness a Priority

You are both ultimately responsible for your happiness. Your partner isn't a mind reader, and neither are you. You're responsible for getting your own needs met, and once you do, you can bring your resulting joy to the relationship as a gift. There is no greater gift you can give yourself and your partner than prioritising yourself and setting up your life to the brim with joy. If you feel misaligned, stuck, or stagnant in your life, you have to be an adult enough to get yourself unstuck through some real efforts. You are the only one that knows where your true bliss lives, capitalise on that and get it exposed.

Give Your Partner Your Full Trust

If you tend to second guess your partner inevitably, he or she will see it and resent you going forward. Instead of questioning every decision, give your partner the benefit of the doubt. Just keep in mind that, the ego and mind love control but the heart doesn't know anything about control. The heart loves and trusts fully.

Be an Initiator

Most men naturally enjoy being the initiators of things. Date nights, sex, adventures, etc. But having this responsibility falling squarely on their shoulders at all times can feel tiresome. In some relationships, the woman has a higher sex drive and she is already used to being the one who initiates. If this is the case for you, this point won't apply as readily to you. You should probably lean back and give your partner space to initiate more often. But in many relationships as per my interactions, the men initiate the majority of the sexual encounters.

The point of choosing to initiate more isn't to swing the pendulum to the opposite side of the spectrum and be the aggressor of all of your future sexual encounters. In that dynamics, you would then take on more of the masculine polarity and it might depolarize your connection rather rapidly. Swinging the pendulum so that you initiate 100% of the sexual encounters won't be ideal, but neither will 0%.

"We attract hearts by the qualities we display but we retain them by the qualities we possess."

Ritu Ghatourey

16

PHYSICAL & EMOTIONAL INTIMACY

The dictionary definition of intimacy is "closeness," describing familiarity or friendship that's close. Intimacy comes in different forms but the notable one for couples in a relationship or marriage is physical or emotional. Sex has become a common reference to intimacy in our modern world. I bet to differ on this assumption because sex is not necessary for intimacy even though it can be part of it. I'm certain by all sense and purpose that sex does not guarantee intimacy. Couples desire happiness but often confuse this desire for happiness with a desire for pleasure and possessions. For instance, having a car can satisfy your desire for pleasure and possessions but can never guarantee you happiness. Our hearts remain restless and discontented until we experience real intimacy. True intimacy is in sharing every aspect of yourself with your partner. This is the greatest gift we can give to our partners; to allow them to simply see us for who we are, with our strengths and weaknesses, flaws, abilities, achievements, and potentials all exposed to them.

Recent data on divorce concludes that intimate relationships have been falling apart for the last few decades. The truth of the matter is that couples have not truly learned or do not know how to sustain pleasure in their respective intimate relationships. The world is not the same as three or two decades ago. I was born into a community with a developed sense of comfort and safety where people felt at home at all times. This network of communities has disintegrated into separate units in isolation. Living in isolation where everyone is minding his own business, or trying to build or salvage a career for a sustainable livelihood makes it difficult to spend as much time as possible together.

It is more important for modern couples to learn, understand, practice, and inculcate intimacy into their relationships. Whether you become physically intimate with your partner or not, you still need to work on building emotional intimacy for your relationship to thrive and remain steadfast. This is true because physical intimacy is not prerequisite to building emotional intimacy. Emotional intimacy on the other hand is necessary to the fulfilment of physical intimacy. Oxytocin is the bonding hormone available to women almost at will. This hormone is rather released to men under two circumstances: *a full-body hug lasting for a few seconds and at orgasm.* The presence of this hormone allows men to feel emotionally connected to their partners.

The continuous dilemma between pleasing yourself and pleasing your partner is what makes relationships hard to navigate. It is not completely ill to turn down your partner's request to meet their physical need but the no's should be few and far between. While a woman has the right to say "No" to an invitation for physical intimacy, the way she handles this affair can have a lasting impact on the relationship. It's never necessary to do anything that is truly unacceptable to you or that may be inconvenient or compromise your emotions negatively. It is also entirely acceptable to sacrifice when necessary to accommodate your partner and his physical needs at will.

Sex is complex and multi-faceted. It's also about procreation; love, connection, and more so, power but can also cause serious problems in a marriage or relationship. While most couples recognize the important role physical intimacy plays in bringing both pleasure and connection, others abuse this precious commodity for their selfish gain. It is undoubtedly factual that positive, healthy sex life can add greatly to a successful relationship and marriage but this should be based on mutual love and respect. Every couple/partner has a right to their physical integrity and therefore should be able to say "no" to sexual advances without fear of repercussions whatsoever.

Male and female sexual desires differ in diverse ways. The sexual desire in men is higher than that of women due to the evolutionary desire to procreate and ensure the survival of the species. But sex, specifically orgasm, is a means for men to feel emotionally close to their partner; hence sexual fulfilment is often seen as an important emotional need for most men. The corresponding emotional need for women is often affection. Human beings have a natural fundamental need to connect through touch. It is the responsibility of each spouse to recognise and lovingly meet their partner's needs for a smooth sailing relationship. Partners who misunderstand such critical differences indicated here and remain insensitive to their better half's needs will open the door for sexual bullying to occur.

Sexual bullying takes many forms and can range from a simple refusal to rape. Pouting, retaliating, withholding, and making yourself unavailable either by direct rejection or not being physically present are also forms of sexual bullying. If your partner indicates a price to pay for not having sex, you may be guilty of unfair practices and subject to abuse. Women who sporadically commit to sex only under special circumstances are also guilty of sexual bullying. No matter who does it, it is an unloving and disrespectful attitude that could put a devastating strain on relationship or marriages.

Couples should understand that physical intimacy is just one component of a healthy relationship. Friendship, trust, fondness, admiration, and commitment on the other hand are the most important elements in a flourishing romantic relationship. Most relationships can survive without intimacy, but neither partner will be happy or feel secure in the relationship. Without happiness and security, relationships will evolve into complications that may reduce the lifespan of the union. Couples need to understand the evolution of relationships to open up the possibility of embracing the changes that come with the maturity of both partners.

Embracing those changes will inevitably lead to the identification of other necessary ways to put a spark to reignite the relationship. The Following Points Will Help You to Form a Profound Connection with Your Partner:

Try to identify why you find it difficult to be intimate with your partner. It could be a result of your upbringing or some other life experience. Growing up in an environment devoid of intimacy can make you develop a cynical attitude towards others. Knowing that which impedes your progress in getting intimate with your partner can be the beginning of finding a lasting solution to ignite the spark.

Allow emotional intimacy to evolve bit by bit more naturally. Forcing things will just disintegrate and blow up in your face. Desist from being too demanding of your partner if you don't want to mess everything up.

Speak languages such as gifts, quality time, words of affirmation, acts of service, and physical touch with your partner.

Allow yourself to be emotionally vulnerable at certain times. This will make you learn how to share your dreams and daily goals together. The more you become emotionally vulnerable and communicate your vulnerability, the greater your chances of building trust.

I must admit though that, one thing I didn't realise when I decided to get married to settle down, is that while settling seems like an enormous act of resignation when you're looking at it from the vantage point of a single person, once you take the initiative and do it, you'll probably be relatively content. It sounds quite obvious to me now, but I didn't fully appreciate back then that what makes for a good marriage isn't necessarily what makes for a good romantic relationship.

Once you're married, it's no more about whom you want to have fun with; it's pretty much about whom you want to manage a household with.

Life partners or some couples sometimes seem to become jaded to the point that they don't believe in, or even crave, romantic connection. But that is not the case; the truth is that their understanding of it simply changes over time and understanding from both partners is the only thing that keeps the spark going unabated.

Dangerous Emotional Abuse Signs

Emotional abuse occurs within and it happens to most of us. It takes many forms and can be difficult to recognise especially during the early stages of friendship or relationships. It becomes obvious when one spends lots of time together as in staying together. Abusers more often than not manipulate their partners into believing that such behaviours are romantic. I have heard some horrible comments from people like "beating is a sign that he loves me". Like seriously, who inflicts pain on a loved one? Such manipulative and misguided statements have contributed to the injury and death of many women. These behaviours are usually a result of jealousy.

Abusers feel justified to subject partners to such barbaric acts as a sign of love and protection. This is dangerous from my understanding, especially considering that the abuser is unable to control his/her feelings and actions. It becomes extremely difficult to escape if the abuse is financially connected in which case the abuser dictates access to financial resources and the victim has no way out. Emotional abuse can often go unnoticed for a long period, with even the victim themselves not realising what is happening to them at times.

The following are certain behaviours that abusers may be convinced or will try to convince you to believe is a romantic stimulant, but are in actual fact toxic and hazardous to the relationship and your life:

Disrespecting Your Personal Space

Respecting the personal space of your partner is one of many romantic things to do in a relationship. If you ask someone to leave you alone and they refuse until you agree to let them in, don't take that for a lovely devotion by any means. A person who loves you will respect your wish to have some alone time and rather make a follow-up later.

Speaking for or Over You in Public

There is nothing as disrespectful and annoying as your partner taking the lead to talk for or over you in public. It's one thing for a person to stand for you and a completely different thing when he acts as your spokesperson in your presence as though you are not competent enough to speak for yourself.

Pressuring You into Having Sex

Sex is graced with a mutual willingness and understanding from both partners. Some people ignorantly assume and believe that happy sex life is an indication of a happy relationship. Coercing your partner to have sex with you at all times is a red flag for abuse. Deliberately withholding sex from your partner as a means of manipulating him/her to submit to something is equally abusive.

Acting Over-Protective

A partner with heavy surveillance on your every move is one hell of a character you cannot ignore. If your partner wants to know your every move, and sometimes outline a strict rule as to whom you see and where you go, take precaution and don't think that will stop after being committed. Such behaviours can only get worse. It's good to have a genuine interest in what happens to and around your partner but overly protective and too much interest in what your partner does with their spare time is a toxic manifestation of abuse.

Turning You against Your Family

When a partner gives you an ultimatum to choose between them and your family at the least provocation, you are in trouble and need to think twice. Abusers have a way of trying to turn a person against their family by creating the impression that your family is not good enough and that they are coming between you.

Questioning Your Sanity, Memory, or Feelings and Calls You Crazy, Insane, and Deny Previous Abuse Ever Happened

Anyone that is made to question his/her sanity is going through gas lighting abuse. This is a type of emotional abuse where power is given to the abuser over the victim. These abusive partners can convince you to stay in the relationship by sowing seeds of self-doubt in your mind such that you become uncertain of your own selective memory.

Unpredictable Affection

A person whose love for you is based on conformity to their needs will resort to withdrawal, aggression, or anger whenever they feel like not having things their way. Such people use affection as a mechanism to manipulate, exploit and control you and the relationship. You always try to go the extra mile in order not to offend them because you don't want to be hurt by their response and actions.

Playing the Guilt Game

People who play the guilt game through the use of threats, self-harm, or suicide as a mechanism to manipulate you to stay in the relationship are dangerous. Subjecting yourself to such people will make you lose your self-esteem and the idea of finding love in another person will appear impossible.

Buying You Gifts to Make Up

You should be-ware of partners who has a habit of only buying you gift when you feel offended. While it is nice to receive a gift from your partner, you must be careful if this happens only or mostly when you have been hurt in one way or the other by that partner. This is because some people avoid addressing issues or resolving conflicts and resort to buying gifts to brush the problem under the carpet, from where it will emerge again in the future.

Constantly Keeping Score

A partner, who keeps score of every wrongdoing to remind you of it and to justify their righteousness, is abusive.

Feeling Trapped

You are under abuse if you feel trapped and helpless in a relationship without any logical way out. This is because the content of ill-treatment has eroded your confidence and self-esteem.

Creating Chaos

Emotionally abusive people create chaos and use it to advance the cause of their abuses. If you recognize some or any of these behaviours or attributes in your partner or relationship, please don't take it lightly. They are commonly highly associated with an emotionally abusive relationship, and just because you are not being physically harmed doesn't mean the abuse isn't taking its toll on you. It is very difficult to free yourself from an abusive partner, but it is very possible to get out if you seek help. Theresa met her husband at the age of 24. He was gainfully employed and he flattered her with his sports car and weekend outings. She was young enough to be flattered by the night outings, constant texting, and calling, but too inexperienced to spot the signs of emotional abuse exhibited even before they tied the knot in a flamboyant traditional wedding a couple of months later.

She said, *"He insults me with claims that I'm either sleeping with my male friends or flirting with his friends.* "He always wanted to be around me so much that I thought it was love. "The insults escalated after our first child. "He called me a worthless and lazy bitch and wouldn't allow me to work. "Any attempt for me to find a job leads to further name-calling and making me feel guilty for attempting to ignore our child. "He calls me constantly when I am out and when I come home early he complains and asks; why are you here this early? "And whether I wasn't having enough fun. "I wanted to be loved so badly I ignored all the pain I was going through. "We had our second child but there was no change in his character. "He constantly told me, I was worthless and that no man will marry me if I left the relationship. "I believed him at some point and I neglected to take care of myself. He will go out and return as he pleases but I was mostly allowed to see friends only in his company or by permission. "After five years of my marital ordeal, he wanted to have another child with me and I refused to give in. "He forced himself on me to accomplish his aim of conceiving. "He wouldn't allow me to talk when he is angry and threatened to kill me if I refuse to have a third child. "I got scared and gave in to his sexual demands but I bought contraceptives from the clinic to prevent any pregnancy. "I got scared of the possibility of him noticing that I was taking contraceptives. I visited my parents one weekend and narrated my ordeal to them and how long it's been going on. "I decided not to return to my husband for fear of his aggressive behaviour until the intervention of my parents. "A month after leaving, I heard he had impregnated another lady in the vicinity."

The real-life story of Theresa shook me hard like an earthquake. The only thing that consoled me was the fact that she enrolled in a

Further Education and Training College to pursue a career towards a National Diploma Qualification.

Her husband's insistent on having another child during the abuse and his approach made her realise the gravity of what she had been enduring and the danger ahead of her. There are so many people like Theresa battling with untold abuse from men and trapped in one way or another without any means of escape. Not many can be lucky enough to escape a torturous relationship as Theresa did after so many years of abuse. Young people are particularly more vulnerable to abuse since they are still naïve to figure out what a healthy relationship is.

Dealing with Emotional and Physical Abuse

Dealing with emotional abuse is something that many people face in relationships on regular basis. The first and most crucial step in dealing with emotional abuse is the ability to spot the signs and the courage to admit and stand up against it. No one deserves to be abused and neither should anyone resort to the use of drugs to cope with its effects. The following will assist you to deal with emotional abuse but it is always necessary to seek professional counselling if you feel your life is in danger:

- o Speak in a calm and clear voice stating your dislike to whatever he/she is doing to you that makes you uncomfortable; "please treat me with dignity and respect." Acting confident in the face of their emotional abuse and keeping your cool will make it harder for your abuser to stand up to you.
- o Do not respond out of emotion; be rational and sensible in your response. Tell him/her that people who care and love each other do not go out of their way to hurt their partners.
- o Change the subject or use humour to distract the person
- o Prioritise your wellbeing and desist from making unimaginable efforts to please your abuser. Take care of yourself through a

healthy lifestyle, eating good food, and get maximum rest to deal with your abusive situation in a good body and a sound mind.

- Try to establish and communicate boundaries you are very sure of keeping. Humbly tell him how much you get hurt by being called names, being yelled at, or disrespected and that if it continues you will report to his/her parents or anyone he looks up to.
- Understand that you cannot change the abusive person by doing something different. Acknowledge your inability to change the abusive partner and that it is their choice to behave abusively. You do not have to blame yourself in any way, but control your response to him/her.
- Start working on an exit plan to leave the relationship. It is advisable to discuss the abusive ordeal with a trusted member of your family or his/her family, church leaders, or a trusted community leader for sound advice because each abusive situation is the same.
- Seek the guidance of a professional if you feel completely lost and even think you are going crazy to some extent.

"Never devalue yourself because someone didn't value you; acknowledge your worth even if no one sees it."

Unknown

17

Your Moral Compass

Mathematician and author of *"The Mathematics of Love"*, Hannah Fry explained that happily ever after comes down to how positive and negative a couple is with each other. In her book, she noted the research of psychologist John Gottman, who studied hundreds of couples and their relationships with their partners, especially in how they responded to each other. It was discovered that couples can be divided into two groups: low-risk and high risk. Couples who are low-risk can have more positive interactions with each other, whereas high-risk couples have the exact opposite. Happy couples see issues within the relationship as unusual, while negative couples don't see issues as anything out of the ordinary. A dictionary definition for armour is a protective covering used to prevent damage from being inflicted on an object or individuals by direct weapons or projectiles through a potentially dangerous activity. Every mission in life requires a certain form of protection to shield one against harm, destruction, and defeat. Weapons can invariably assist one to therefore become victorious in an activity, event, or real-life situation.

For instance, becoming a professional athlete require consistent effort and sacrifices. Competition is tense and only the most dedicated athletes get to play professionally and survive. Sports may build social characters such as teamwork, self-sacrifice, and loyalty as armours of excelling in a sporting career. But they do not build the moral character of athletes from a moral idealistic standpoint. We have seen great athletes with extraordinary talent fall as a result missing pertinent armours of morals in their career and life as a whole. The moral compass of a person is his/her ability to judge what is right and wrong and act accordingly. Our moral compass simply points us in the right direction.

We might have different definitions of right and wrong but our moral compass at the end of it all provides an objective standard. It goes beyond making us see what is right and wrong. It also directs our actions towards that which is good for the greater good even if it may not be beneficial for us. Without our moral compasses as humans, it becomes very easy to just do whatever is convenient to us without consideration of whether it is right or wrong. People without a moral compass find it easy to stretch the truth whenever it benefits them or do things without thinking of the consequences for others and society. They become selfish, greedy monsters who only care about their own needs and wants.

According to Dr. Todd Hall, all human beings are born with a moral compass. We all have that innate sense of what is right and wrong. As we grow older, those instincts may grow or fade or become so twisted and corrupted. There are quite several effective and top-notch athletes who blew away their successful careers due to behaviours and decisions that were devoid of moral considerations. The demise of these athletes and sporting personalities were as a result of over-reliance on their efficiencies without a real moral compass. Losing touch with your moral compass makes you extinct to the feelings of others far or near. The wisdom of God that empowers you to efficiently overcome temptations and deal with issues diligently leaves your human body if you don't have a space within you to accommodate it. You become vulnerable in the absence of a moral compass, rendering you further vulnerable to commit regrettable atrocities against humanity through incautious decisions. A close look at the careers of these personalities will give you an explicit attestation of people who lost their moral compass and made decisions and choices based on their own will and efficiency. The results of their endeavours were simply bewildering.

Aaron Hernandez

He was a rising star tight end for the New England Patriots and a 2011 Pro Bowl selection with a five-year contract in 2012 worth $40 million.

He's been charged with murder in the shooting death of a 27-year-old semipro football player Odin Lloyd. If convicted, he will get life in prison without parole.

Oscar Pistorius

Six months after proving to the world that he could race on blades and compete with able-bodies athletes, the South African double-amputee sprinter was charged in the shooting death of his girlfriend, model Reever Steenkamp.

Lance Armstrong

He was a hero, fighter, and icon. He beat cancer and amazed the world by winning the Tour de France titles. The seven-time Tour de France Champion has stripped off all his Tour titles, lost his endorsement deal with Nike, and admitted to doing an emotional interview with Oprah Winfrey.

Different experts give different reasons why relationships and marriages fail; from financial pressures to unrealistic expectations. But one lethal weapon that should be evident in relationships and marital lives for peace and love to prevail is an active moral compass. Whether you like it or not, as soon as you commit to a lifetime relationship with a partner, you are joined in a spiritual battle. There will always be invisible warfare going on in your life and if the assaults of the enemy become successful then your union will not reproduce a Godly heritage and you will disintegrate in no time. But there is hope if and only if we correctly and diligently develop a moral compass to guard our actions and inactions. Like many of the athletes who fail themselves and society by committing a heinous crime against humanity at the expense of their ones flourishing career, the most common mistake we make at some point during our relationships is not "reading" our Moral Compass. By "reading" I mean using our mind to understand how our values might affect our decisions.

After reading our moral compass we need to "use it" to make ethically informed decisions. The difficulty lies in using what we read to make ethical decisions. Most people sometimes read their compass, hear that important little voice in their mind, but make a decision that takes them in a direction opposite to the one recognised by their values.

People Fail to Follow Their Innate Core Values When Confronted with Challenges Because:

They think their ethical choice would have challenging short-term side effects on their relationships. It might create more disagreement or conflict for them and their relationship. For example, I have seen couples avoid talking with a partner engaging in some very bad behaviour because they were afraid of conflict or were afraid their partners would leave them. People also choose to violate their values because of the benefits the opposite decision brings them. This is very dangerous to couples because it will have the greatest impact on relationship viability. The most important aspect of having a moral compass is to use it. If you develop a good moral compass and then ignore its readings, it will be of no benefit to you. To read your moral compass accurately is to simply logically consider your choices in a given situation, making sure your internal ethics and values are in agreement with the decisions you make. When you first develop an interest in someone and starts dating, your main focus typically is whether there's chemistry and some witty common interests between you and your newfound love. The fun times can easily last for few months, but soon one of you or both of you will start to wonder whether what you have is enough or more is needed.

While a great friendship is a solid start to creating a stable long-term relationship, we sometimes forget that commitment, honest communications, mutual trust and respect for each other's boundaries are also vital to nourish the relationship. Love is simply not enough to guarantees a good relationship. You need to share a vision for the future as a couple, you need to agree on finances, and you need to develop a path to merge your lives into a complete household.

It's worth acknowledging that, no one is perfect, and the older we get the more baggage we all carry. However, there is a big difference between a one-time genuine flaw in judgment and a long-standing history of poor choices. For example, anyone can make a mistake in their choice of a partner in the past, but that is very different from a person that has racked up years of multiple failed relationships. Many might have a one-time indiscretion towards the end of their relationship, but that is nothing compared to consistent sordid woes created by a chronic cheat whose sense of entitlement will always overshadow the needs of other people. Romantic relationships come with a hefty risk of broken hearts, so it is necessary to pay very calculated attention to your partner's moral compass. Use these wise words from Kenny Rogers in The Gambler as your guide: know when to hold them, know when to fold them, know when to walk away, and know when to run.

A colleague of mine married to a caring and beautiful lady confronted me with an issue one fine holiday over a drink. He said, Richard, it seems I am missing my ex. I don't know what is wrong with me. He continued, my ex and I dated for some time before I got married. We didn't break up but we just went our separate ways because of distance when she was transferred to another province for work purposes. We met after some time when I was still engaged to my wife and then rekindled our relationship without my engaged woman's knowledge.

    I got married later in the year and got over her to concentrate on my marriage life and aspirations. She sent me a text that she can't get over our past and will always cherish the memories. She sent me texts to take me back to the feelings I had for her. She requested for us to have a go at it again and that whatever we do can be our little secret. She was the one I pictured myself marrying, but I thought she had forgotten about me. I am not sure why I am feeling like this. I do need your input for a direction. As shocking as that revelation was, I gathered my composure to quickly think on my feet whilst gulping some fine whiskey down my throat. What came to mind after listening to him was a "moral compass".

    I ask him, have you ever seen a defective compass? Him: yes! A defective pocket compass can pretty well show some directions, but it can't be trusted near the magnetic pole. It often points in any direction, confusing north with south and east with west. That is where you find yourself now, and that is where most people in similar situations find themselves. A defective relationship compass is without any sense of direction. Your ex-girlfriend/boyfriend had all the chances to claim and be with you before you met your wife/husband and got married to her. Now all he/she has to offer you is a night of fantasy by asking you to commit adultery with him/her. All he/she is saying is, I am available for sex and you are tempted to jump onto the train.

    You are undoubtedly starved for something if you are in this situation and your utmost task is to figure out what it is. Your only way out is to reset your moral compass to work effectively to assist in making decisions that will by no means negatively affect your relationship with your significant half. If you can't fix your compass to get over your ex with the right decision, then you are not worth a husband/wife to anyone. Divorce is painful, but so is betrayal. Do not by any sense and purpose take a good partner down this path with you because of your faulty moral compass. Peter Drucker advises, "Do not knowingly harm." I think knowing how to read and use your moral compass will help you make better ethical decisions in your relationships.

Being morally upright in integrity is critical for building trust with your partner and creating the solid relationships great marriages and unions thrive on. Not everyone has an effective moral compass with integrity. There are clear warning signs that a person you're dealing with probably won't do the right thing given the chance. It's up to you to detect the following signs to decide on your fate before it's too late:

Lack of Forgiveness

They usually don't see the value in giving the benefit of the doubt to others. They offer second chances rarely, if at all but make mistakes themselves and expect to be forgiven. I know people who believe that there is no such thing as right or wrong and that people's feelings must simply be honoured. But, what if I feel like taking something that doesn't belong to me or spew hatred to a particular individual or group of people because they are different from me. People are separated from their moral compass in recent generations and centuries. It is therefore difficult to find partners with the same values but the reality is that human beings are largely guided by their morals and therefore we need to reposition ourselves to develop each other along the lines of valuable morals for the benefit of collective coexistence. If you want to stay on the same path towards a lasting relationship then your values must in one way or the other complement each other, otherwise, you will be drifted in different directions in no time. A healthy relationship requires your compass pointing in the same direction as your partner's. If your moral compasses are taking you in different directions then you're simply not going to get to the same destination together.

A few years ago, before I got married, I radically shifted the way I approached dating, especially how I determine if I liked someone and if I was willing to take it further. I moved away from a good romantic match based on looks to a new system of focusing on my date's level of consciousness or self-awareness.

I used my moral compass to pay attention to my intuitive voice. That led me into looking deeper beyond my arbitrary list of character traits and superficialities that are only good at satisfying my ego to one that deals with eating into the consciousness of my date to see if they are worth my time. Consciousness and self-awareness are all about trying to figure out if our potential partner is emotionally mature, his/her perspective on life, his/her mind-set, and how the person handles challenges. This is a level of state of assessment and life is not easy to reach but very possible to attain too. The difficulty lies in the fact that you will have to let go off your pertinent requirements that satisfy your immediate romantic needs to expand your perception of what you consider attractive. This confirms that, while physical appearance and characteristics are an integral part of dating, they are not in any way the priority. The level of consciousness of your potential partner will determine if your relationship will be successful. The other important but difficult thing to do is how to successfully assess your potential partner's level of consciousness and moral compass direction. To achieve that:

Listen Attentively

Some people become too excited when a suitor honour's their date. They get busy trying to impress each other so much that they miss the vital clues that are unleashed about people's real attributes, including moral values, goals, and general objectives in life and relationships at large. Don't ignore your instinct and discovery: There are quite some charming and attractive people out there without an iota of what it takes to be in a relationship. It is tempting to overlook obvious signs in a potential partner because of the excitement of dating someone you have been longing and praying for, but people always show us who they are. We simply have to listen to our instinct attentively. Even though not everyone draws their sense of right and wrong from religion, there is some sort of universal code most people follow.

I have my sense of morality based on the laws of cause and effect. If I don't want to experience being lied to, I shouldn't lie. If I don't want to be stolen from, then I shouldn't steal too. Whilst this is true, people feel that to find love or keep someone around, they have to compromise what they feel is right. They believe that little exceptions won't matter much, but those are the things that always lead to bigger and complicated ones. Human beings have a sense of right and wrong, a fine innate ability to know what is good and what isn't. Not honouring your inner compass creates guilt, and negative situations you'd rather not attempt to find yourself in. We all make mistakes, but compromising your values and morals won't make you happy, and in the end, it won't secure you the love you so yearn for.

Let's Look at This Real-Life Scenario

You are the head of a home and there is an opportunity to make some extra cash for your company through some scheme that will increase your income to also help your family. It is not illegal but it may be unethical or encourage fraudulent behaviour going forward. Your partner is excited by your idea as well as your CEO and they have encouraged you to follow through.

You have one of two choices, *a Choice without moral compass and Choice with a moral compass.* **First:** You strategically weigh your decision to find out whether the personal and professional risk is worth the possible riches and respect. In this instance, your rational thought is suppressed by your emotional & mental state (lust for wealth and fear of disapproval). You are somewhat blind to the emotional and long-term risk and confused by the idea of missing an opportunity. You are practically in fear of missing out on an opportunity more than you value the idea of a wise decision.

You then proceed to make a rash decision being half-blind to the consequences ahead. **Second:** You strategically weigh your decision with guidance that transcends the situation. You experience emotional & mental influences (lust, fear, and irrational thoughts). You decide to take time to reflect and revisit the ethos that informs your decision-making. This enables you to see the potential for unethical and illegal acts and to further imagine the destruction and pain you could find yourself in. You listen to your instinct and affirm what your conscience has been telling you; this opportunity is a mistake with series of consequences.

As a person with the power, you need to have authority over your decision-making process and a moral compass to stabilize that process. This helps to balance the influences of your emotional state, psychological flaws, and social pressures. Our moral compasses need intermittent calibration. If you take a well-functioning compass and put it in a room with an electromagnet, it will forget which way is north. It'll point to the electromagnet because the electromagnet will be exerting far more powerful force than that exercised by the distant North Magnetic Pole. It cannot ignore the electromagnetic force of attraction. In the same way, every problematic relationship exerts a force that can alter your attitude, change your course, and make you forget yourself and your values. You can't do anything without checking with the relationship first to get rid of that interference to calibrate your compass.

For the moral compass to work properly, you must forget the needs and requirements of the relationship for as long as it takes to connect with yourself and recognize what is important. This means that, if you have somehow lost yourself, you need to try to find yourself. In the meantime, thoughts of reconciliation should become secondary, whilst you focus on personal peace. Ever tried to calibrate an ordinary compass? You will realise that, for a minute or two, the needle will spin around aimlessly until it finds magnetic north. The danger here is that you will be completely lost and confused in the process if you try to rely on it for direction.

Sometimes when people free themselves of the effects of a certain toxic relationship, for a few days they feel similarly lost and confused. They often feel as though they've lost their bearings. They don't know what's important anymore because they've been separated from their values for far too long living someone else's values of life. Many end up having their lives dictated by the relationship because it's more familiar and comfortable. But to remain free of the effects of a dysfunctional relationship, it's important to stay with the process of calibration long enough so that you can get your bearings straight. You have to reconnect with your values by finding them behind your emotions, renewing your faith, exploring spiritual practices, determining what has meaning and purpose for your life, and reminding yourself of the things you told yourself you would never do.

One significant thing about your moral compass is that it can tell you the general direction of whatever is significant to you, but it can't be certain of how to get there. Your topographical features of a destination are also worth considering as you travel. You can't head straight in a certain direction all the time because your compass directs you there. You must consider the availability of mountains, rivers, or an ocean that may get in your way. The compass direction is one thing; the path you take is another. You may have more than one thing you value in some instances, but the perfect path will take you to all of them as expected. What I am driving at is that your moral compass points to a very particular direction, but there are infinite routes that can take you there. Therefore, insist on your values, but don't get so blinded by which path you take that you overlook the alternatives available to you.

18

Love Personified
(The very definition of love)

Love is not an abstract concept without a meaningful expression. Love is real and serves a significant purpose in one's life. The virtues of true love should be manifested in the life of every human being. Love is the best feeling of expression in the world. We fall into it, seek, cherish it, and share it. It's a language of expression that everyone can understand, regardless of race, colour, gender, and status. As universally acceptable as it is, it's also quite a complex and powerful emotion to define. Our partners play a vital part in our desire for companionship and love, but they also serve as a daily experience to lay ourselves down. [Quote: *"If I speak in the tongues of men and angels, but have not love, I am only a resounding gong or a clanging cymbal"*] Similarly, you can say the nicest things ever and shower your partner with gifts and romance but without True love, all that will be in vain.

People may come into your life with goodies and say all the sweet things and promises you want to hear but with a common selfish objective of only exploring your body. After that objective is achieved, they begin to show less interest and reveal their true identity. Character is like a cork; you can't suppress it, it will always find its way up afloat. A gift without love is "nothing." We misplace our priorities if we measure our significance by the things we possess or give to our partners. This is a special warning for those who think luring people with a gift can buy them their love, and equally important to those who follow material things as evidence of love. Everything you do for your partner must be directed by love. The word love needs a thorough diagnosis when it comes to its definition.

It is mostly used according to its first definition given in the dictionary: "an intense feeling of deep affection." In other words, love is what one feels if I am right. I am convinced that, love should not merely be seen as a feeling but as an enacted emotion. This is because to love is actually to feel and to act lovingly. I have seen bruises on women suffered by their partners. And I am certain you may have witnessed abuses in different forms or been a victim of abuse from a partner whom you claim to love. Since they see love as a feeling, the truth of the real meaning of love, which is that you do not love someone whom you repeatedly beat and abuse eludes them. You may have very strong feelings about them, you may even believe you cannot live without them, but you do not love them if you manhandle them.

When my first child was born, my first reaction to her, a person who so recently did not exist was that "I would do anything for her." The love was effortless and to say I will do anything for her is to act on my feelings. That is why we often hear the phrase "you don't act as you love me." We know in our bones that love is not a feeling alone, but a feeling that flows into action. Love is a relational word among humans. It is possible to love things or objects that do not love you back but the love of a human being is directional and reciprocal. There is a lover and a beloved. Love in its real sense is not about the feelings of the lover; it is not egotism. It is when one person believes in another person and shows it in action by protecting her from all forms of internal and external forces. Though love can tie you to another person, it shouldn't keep you in a cage. It should allow you to flourish in all facets of life, both independently and as a couple. In the end, you are the best decision-maker as to what love means within the context of your relationships, and there is no "right way" to define what love is or what it should be. As long as both of you act on your feelings towards each other and your most important needs are being met without "visible and invisible bruises" then that's a good thing.

One of the most important qualities of true love is respect that is mutually felt between partners. Respect, by all sense and purpose, supersedes lust and romantic love. Once you find out that you are loathing your significant half because you feel like you are finally seeing them for who they truly are, then that is a sure sign that the love spell is diminishing. For us to understand the real meaning and essence of love, we have to make effort to understand what prevents us from loving unconditionally. Sometimes, our judgments about someone can make us angry, disappointed, resentful, and even separated from that person. Those are some of the things that impede our ability to the people in our lives. For instance, you might experience thought about how your partner isn't appreciative enough, not in good shape, not supportive, etc. and these thoughts just get in the way of the expression of love. The fulfilment we seek in life comes from giving love, and not from receiving it.

We Often Mistake the Following as Love and End up Not Getting the Fulfilment We Expect in Life

If you expect your significant half to do things for you, at that moment, it's not necessarily love. Ever heard of this "If you love me, you will do this and that for me". Now, when you try to get your partner to sacrifice and fill your needs just to make you happy, it often breeds burden and suffering. Of course, if you love someone, your sacrifice to their plight is not regarded as a sacrifice, but a real joy. But, where one is forced or guilt tricked to do something they don't want to willingly do then love is missing in action. If you love them, you won't ask them to do something they don't also want to do because it makes it look like, at the moment you are only concern about what you want.

Types of Love

Eros love: It is described as erotic and sexual love. Eros love is the physical, sensual intimacy between a husband and wife. Eros love is part of God's design, a gift of his goodness for procreation and enjoyment. Sex is a source of delight and a beautiful blessing to be shared between married couples. (Proverbs 5:18–19, ESV) Let your fountain be blessed, and rejoice in the wife of your youth, a lovely deer, and a graceful doe. Let her breasts fill you at all times with delight; be intoxicated always in her love. This type of love is that which permeates the lives of married couples.

Storge love: It refers to family love and is described as fondness born out of familiarity or dependency. People in a romantic relationship often expect unconditional Storge, but find only the need and dependency of Eros, and sometimes the maturity and fertility of philia. Eros then mutate into Storge as time progresses in the life of couples. Storge is a very strong love element because it combines both Eros and philia. Once you get married, you exhibit brotherly affectionate love to your partner (philia) and equally engage in erotic and sexual love (Eros).

Philia love: It refers to brotherly friendship and affectionate love. Aristotle believed that a person can bear goodwill to another for one of three reasons: that he is useful; that he is pleasant; and, above all, that he is good, that is, rational and virtuous. Relationships founded on goodness are associated not only with mutual benefit but also with companionship, dependability, and trust.

Agape love: It is universal love. Agape does not depend on filiation or familiarity. It encompasses the modern concept of altruism, defined as unselfish concern for the welfare of others. Agape helps to build and maintain the psychological, social, and environmental fabric that shields, sustains, and enriches us in a relationship with each other.

Ludus: Ludus is playful or uncommitted love involving activities such as teasing and dancing, or more overt flirting, seducing, and conjugating. The focus is largely on fun, and sometimes also on conquest, with no strings attached. It is casual, undemanding, and uncomplicated, and can be very long-lasting.

Pragma: Pragma is a practical love founded on reason or duty and one's longer-term interests. Sexual attraction in this case takes a back seat in favour of personal qualities and compatibilities, shared goals, and making it work. Most relationships that start as Eros or Ludus end up as various combinations of Storge and pragma.

Philautia: Philautia is self-love, which can be healthy or unhealthy. It becomes unhealthy if one places him/herself above others or the greater good. Healthy self-love is akin to self-esteem, which is our cognitive and, above all, emotional appraisal of our own worth relative to that of others.

The seven descriptions of love as illustrated above needs to be in one way or the other evidently in both partners of a relationship to build a solid foundation of union that will stand the test of time. There is no better exercise for spiritual development than marrying someone and constantly working to serve one another. You need the patience to allow your faith in a relationship to mature to produce hope. Hope will get you to the end goal, which is success in the relationship. Couples should be optimistic at all times, looking forward to a lovely relationship.

Trials are a fact of living in this fallen world, so couples need to learn how to handle problems. It is very common for certain couples to look upon themselves as wiser as and better than their partners in deceit. Such an attitude is self-deceiving because pretending to be what you do not put a strain upon yourself and the relationship, and sooner or later will find the sad effects. Each couple is supposed to prove his/her work because the better we know our hearts and ways, the less we will despise others, and the more we will be disposed to help them under physical and mental weaknesses or shortfalls.

19

WHY RELATIONSHIP FAILS

Relationships are a single attribute that we cannot live without. It is a complex entity that things which attracted couples to each other can with time become irritating enough to drive them apart. Being able to have a lasting connection is pretty difficult for most people in relationships and cracks may be developed without noticing. The seemingly unnoticeable cracks eat into the fibre of the relationship and partners begin to notice not so good long-term future together. At this point, only one person takes the action by in most cases walking out of the one's enviable union.

The best chance available at achieving an ever-lasting relationship is by understanding the main reason most relationships come to an end. This can help you spot warning signs on time, and reflect on your behaviour and attitudes to determine whether they are negative or positive energy to the relationship.

As we grow older, we realize that love isn't as easy as the movies portray it to be. Everything always seems to work out to expectation with a reasonable end in a fantasyland. But when it comes to real-life situations, relationships just aren't that easy. But real-life relationships don't necessarily have to be difficult. It's the people in the relationship that make things difficult. Keeping a relationship alive requires some serious determination and inspiration. It goes beyond simply staying attracted or feeling the spark between you and your partner because of promises you have made to each other.

It is common knowledge that everyone in a relationship for the right reasons yearns to achieve a "forever" with partners, and the first step to achieve that is by being handy with the reasons most relationships fail. If you acknowledge that anything in this book talks to your situation, then reassess what you think a healthy relationship should look like.

Then apply the necessary adjustment for a better future relationship endeavour. Infidelity is a deal-breaker for most couples but some are also able to survive it for some reason. To others, it leads to loss of interest in physical intimacy, constant criticism, and defensiveness that are not healthy to a formidable and happy relationship. Some people can walk away from years of marriage without any problem whatsoever whereas a few days out of a relationship can trigger emotional trauma that lingers for years in others.

Whilst there are natural reasons that can lead to relationship failure, there are pretty much lots of avoidable reasons that will cause a relationship to fail. It's inevitable that your romantic partner will come with traits or beliefs contrary to which you approve. But, will that be enough reason to leave your partner in the search for a perfect match? I don't think so. What matters most is how you understand and relate to these differences.

Kingsley believes in healthy eating and regular exercise. After engaging Sally and moving in with her, he realised that she has a sweet tooth and is not a fun exercise. Kingsley enjoys the availability of little snacks provided by Sally and the fact that she is always available at home on weekends without unnecessary outings. With time, he became frustrated each time she grabs a piece of chocolate and decline to go to the gym and aerobics at the park with him. As his frustration grew, he tried to change her habit. He started by complaining of not having enough money to budget for ice cream, chocolate, cookies, and all the goodies that she so much adores at her leisure.

Sally finds her means to purchase confectioneries because she is a working woman with income. Kinsley started making comments about her body and how it's looking out of shape, each time she finds her munching on some sweet snack. He hardly saw his actions as problematic because he thought he was trying to help her change her lifestyle to benefit her by living a much healthier life. This happens to a lot of people in a relationship. As time progresses, this avoidable active attempts to change your partner will naturally cause anger and resentment leading to unnecessary arguments of defence and counter arguments that will eventually become disastrous.

The need for adjustment of a certain trait of character that is not healthy for your partner can be done through a point of acceptance. You have to accept your partner as he/she is then that sense of acceptance can be interpreted as trust and love which will lay the foundation for change if any.

When you don't trust someone, you don't feel comfortable with them and they will feel attacked and resent to anything you say about them.

Jasper met a beautiful first-year university student in Pretoria. She travelled overseas for holidays after a while. Whilst there, she sent a message to Jasper: "hey, I just wanted to let you know that I have got an awesome guy and want you to move on." This experience scared the hell out of him, and he struggled to trust women for years. His lack of trust manifested in various ways by trying not to be vulnerable, overreacting to girlfriends talking with other guys, and jumping out of relationships with the least provocation before he got hurt. Failure to trust his partners due to his previous experience unconsciously sabotaged most of his adult romantic relationships and hindered his ability to build enduring relationships. Jasper's problem is a lack of trust, of course, due to his experience but you can't look at everyone with the same lens. And while you may be able to move past the strange ways in which a lack of trust manifests in the short-term, in the long run, it will kill your relationship.

Eventually, your partner will tire of your inability to trust them, and the relationship will break down. If you struggle to trust your partner, especially when he or she hasn't done anything that directly or indirectly violate your trust, you need to identify the source of your mistrust. Lack of trust in most cases emanate from fear of being hurt, which can come from childhood experiences, witness to trust issues in family and friends, personal experiences. Regardless of the cause, it is always possible to rebuild your sense of trust by taking lessons from your past experiences and moving on as a new leaf. The first few months or years of a relationship are interestingly awesome without many hurdles but once nature takes a seat, you will inevitably run into challenges.

To navigate and endure these challenges that most often come naturally due to us being humans, you need to be able to communicate well with your partner. Eric had a promotion at work that came with the opportunity to manage a multi-million project. His fiancée shared the excitement with him over dinner and promised to support him all-out. But as the project progresses, she noticed that he is spending much more time at work than with her. She started to wonder if Eric cares about work more than her and their relationship. Your ability to maintain a healthy relationship largely relies on your ability to communicate your emotions, beliefs, and needs carefully to your partner in such situations. She was unable to communicate her frustration to her partner productively and rather ended up doing things that will escalate the problem. She responded to her frustration by being short-tempered and making arguments over small issues.

This compounded the problem and Eric started thinking that she doesn't support his pursuit to succeed in his career anymore. You have to learn to communicate your emotions calmly and honestly from a place of genuine understanding so that you can handle the challenges more appropriately. Instead of lashing out at your partner, you should tell them that you feel that due to their focus on work for which you genuinely understand, they are not meeting your needs. An open discussion of how a certain situation is affecting you without assuming that it is a direct aspersion to you will make way for a healthy communication channel that will allow you to find a productive path forward.

Dr. John Gottman of the University of Washington, a foremost expert on couple's studies, concluded after over twenty years of research that the single, best predictor of divorce is when one or both partners show contempt in the relationship. Contempt, the opposite of respect, is often expressed via negative judgment, criticism, or sarcasm regarding the worth of an individual. This can be translated as being "tough on the person and soft on the issue". This destroys can destroy the well-being of any relationship like wildfire.

The last thing people in a relationship want to think about is a break-up but the reality is that it happens all the time. Love conquers everything, but if there's one thing that can't be conquered by love then it's when couples are not on the same page. According to Lesli Doares, a certified relationship coach in Cary, North Carolina, "67 percent of disagreements in a relationship never get resolved and they don't need to, but the other 33 percent, if not resolved, can lead to the end of the relationship." she notes that these so-called "deal-breakers" are often "desires of one partner for the relationship to get more serious, personal beliefs and values, the kind of lifestyle each person wants to live and wanting to have children."

Some people avoid conflict and pretend that issue in their relationship is non-existing because they live in fear of being alone. However, such a strategy is not sustainable, and sooner or later the conflicts will rear their ugly heads and it's usually too late to solve them constructively.

Accepting relationships irrespective of how unhealthy they are is another common pattern that leads to failed relationships. Couples tend to be honest and open about their personal feelings and emotions during the early days of a relationship. As time progress many automatically assume that their significant half should be able to read their body language and just know what's on their mind. Great relationships don't happen out of the vacuum but take years of practice and missteps to build the kind of relationship that looks effortless and worth emulating from the outside.

The reality is that the longer you're together, the easier it becomes to take your partner for granted, and the things you once did to maintain a healthy and romantic relationship start to wane. The good news is that it's never too late to turn things around regardless of how old you are or how long you have been in a relationship. In other to strengthen your relationship, you need to be vulnerable, honest, and understanding with your partner.

Expressing your vulnerability in front of your spouse is rarely comfortable or easy but doing so is an essential component of a healthy relationship. Comparing your relationship to everyone else's relationship is a highway to failure. By comparing yourself, you are only going to feel worse and ultimately master the act of sabotaging your relationship instead of saving it. The grass is greener where you water it and no relationship is as flawless as it looks especially on social media space.

20

History of Marriage

Though marriage has ancient roots, recently love had little to do with it. The first recorded evidence of marriage ceremonies uniting one woman and one man dates from about 2350 B.C., in Mesopotamia. Marriage then evolved into a widespread institution embraced by the ancient Hebrews, Greeks, and Romans over the years. But back then, marriage had little to do with love or with religion. Marriage's primary purpose was to bind women to men, and thus guarantee that a man's children were truly his biological heirs. Through marriage, a woman became a man's property. In the betrothal ceremony of ancient Greece, a father would hand over his daughter with these words: "I pledge my daughter for producing legitimate offspring." Among the ancient Hebrews, men were free to take several wives; married Greeks and Romans were free to satisfy their sexual urges with concubines, prostitutes, and even teenage male lovers, while their wives were required to stay home and tend to the household. If wives failed to produce offspring, their husbands could give them back and marry someone else.

As the Romans and their church became a powerful institution in Europe, the blessings of a priest became a necessary step for a marriage to be legally recognized. By the eighth century, marriage was widely accepted in the Catholic Church as a sacrament, or a ceremony to bestow God's grace. At the Council of Trent in 1563, the sacramental nature of marriage was written into canon law. There was some improvement in how women are seen and treated and men were trained to show maximum respect to their wives, and divorce was forbidden. The doctrine of Christianity declared that "the two shall be one flesh," giving husband and wife access to each other's bodies.

In the past, couples were brought together for practical reasons, and not necessarily because they fell in love. As time progressed, many marriage partners felt deep mutual love and devotion. The idea of romantic love in itself, as a motivating force for marriage, only goes came into effect during the middle Ages. Many scholars also believe that the concept was invented by the French. Twelfth-century advice literature told men to woo the object of their desire by praising her eyes, hair, and lips. In the 13th century, Richard de Fournival, physician to the king of France, wrote "Advice on Love," in which he suggested that a woman cast her love flirtatious glances-"anything but a frank and open entreaty." Marilyn Yalom, a Stanford historian and author of A History of the Wife, credits the concept of romantic love with giving women greater leverage in what had been a largely pragmatic transaction. Wives no longer existed solely to serve men. The history of marriage customs in Africa takes three principal forms. Marriage customs in other parts of the world have patterns that were/are similar to the history of marriage customs in Africa.

Marriage by Capture

During the wedding festivities, friends of the couple may kidnap the bride and will release her only after the groom negotiates for, and pays her ransom. The kidnapping can be done multiple times throughout the wedding ceremony and it is up to the groom to notice when his bride goes missing. In other communities, the groom's family and friends abduct the bride. Once the abduction is known, the groom's "posse" and the bride's "posse" meet halfway between their villages (or halfway between their family compounds if they are from the same village), where they will either engage in a mock battle OR exchange gifts and/or payment for the bride. Such practices are seen among the Ganda/Bantu tribes of Uganda and the people of Nyanza in Kenya.

Marriage by Purchase

The theory behind this is simply the same but there are subtle differences from tribe to tribe in Africa when it comes to the actual execution. In Zaire, the groom brings two copper rings or an arrow to the bride and her family. Upon acceptance of the gifts, the couple becomes officially betrothed. Several gifts are exchanged during the actual wedding ceremony including a knife given by the groom to the bride's father. The knife signifies that the new husband is now responsible for the wife's safety and well-being. Among the Zulu, the groom gives cattle to the bride's family and father. The theory behind the cattle is that if for any reason the marriage doesn't work out and the bride has to return to her family, the cattle serve as insurance for her so that she will be able to support herself.

Marriage by Choice

This is also known as a "love match". This type of marriage is a move away from marriages in which the prospective couples play no role in spouse selection. This shift is fuelled by rising levels of education, growing urbanisation, and increasing age at marriage. Throughout most of history, romantic love was not considered a suitable basis for marriage. Marriages were typically arranged by families through negotiations designed to increase wealth, property, or prestige, establish ties, or gain political advantages. In modern individualistic societies, on the other hand, romantic love is seen as the essential basis for marriage.

Neuroscience describes romantic love as one of the central brain systems that have evolved to ensure mating, reproduction, and the perpetuation of the species (Fisher, 1992). Romantic love manifests seemingly as an involuntary, passionate longing for another person where people experience obsessiveness, craving, possessiveness, anxiety, and compulsive, intrusive thoughts. Even though romantic love is often characterized as an involuntary force that sweeps people off their feet, choosing a mate involves an implicit or explicit cost/benefit analysis that affects who a person falls in love with.

Contemporary Marriage

Marriage has largely evolved into a universal phenomenon within different societies and cultures. This is attributed to the many basic social and personal functions for which structure such as sexual gratification and regulation, division of labour between the sexes, economic production and consumption, and satisfaction of personal needs for affection, status, and companionship are provided. For many in these contemporary times, the strongest function of marriage concerns procreation, the care of children, their education, socialization, and livelihoods at large. Marriage has evolved in different forms over the years. The nature of marriage in Western countries particularly in this 21st century with regards to the significance of procreation and the ease of divorce has had some drastic changes.

For instance, in April 2001 the Netherlands became the first country to legalize same-sex marriages. Countries including Canada followed in 2005, France in 2013, the United States in 2015, and Germany in 2017. In 2006, South Africa became the first African country to legalize same-sex marriage, with a constitution that also protects against discrimination based on sexual orientation. In contemporary societies, individuals choose their mates and dating has become the most typical way for people to meet and become acquainted with prospective partners.

Successful dating may result in courtship, which then leads to marriage. In Judaism marriage is believed to be instituted by God and is described as making the individual complete. The modern ceremony begins with the groom signing the marriage contract before a group of witnesses. The groom is led to the bride's room, where he places a veil on her followed by the ceremony under the huppa (a canopy that symbolizes the bridal bower), which involves the reading of the marriage contract, the seven marriage benedictions, the groom's placing a ring on the bride's finger. After the ceremony, the couple is led into a private room for seclusion, which symbolizes the consummation of the marriage. Most Christians consider it a permanent union based upon mutual consent. Christian weddings have taken place before a priest or minister, and the ceremony involves the exchange of vows, readings from Scripture, a blessing, and, sometimes, the Eucharistic rite.

Islamic marriages are not strictly a sacrament but they are always understood as a gift from God or service to God. The basic Islamic tenets concerning marriage are laid out in the Qur'ān, which states that the marital bond rests on "mutual love and mercy" and that spouses are "each other's garments." Muslim men are allowed to have up to four wives at one time, but the wives must all be treated equitably. Marriages are traditionally contracted by the father or guardian of the bride and her intended husband, who must offer his bride the mahr, a payment offered as a gift to guarantee her financial independence. British colonial rule in Africa tried to eradicate our customary marriage, but the independence of Africans has led to its re-emergence, although certain formal requirements such as registration are maintained at certain places.

In South Africa, a customary marriage is entered into following the traditions and customs of indigenous African customary law. There exist certain requirements that must be complied with to conclude a valid customary marriage.

21

HONOURING YOUR PARTNER

We are in an era of increased pseudo-intimacy where couples are quick at jumping over the challenges and dedication that a deep relationship requires. In this era, friends who are not officially dating may exchange pleasantries and hang out at ungodly hours resulting in unhealthy and unintended emotional attachment. Women are considered more relational than men and therefore stand a chance of falling deep for a relationship leading to a commitment that one has not given much thought to. This is why most relationships end abruptly and explains why women are the most disappointed and hurt in most cases. A relationship that starts without the proper order of things involving time to know someone to build a friendship before graduating to engage in physical affections intended for committed relationships and marriage is subject to failure. You can engage in a friendship that involves a growing emotional intimacy but without the proper commitment, sacrifices, and required maturity to shoulder the responsibilities of what comes after the state of ecstasy, you will be staring in the face of untold pain and disappointment sooner than anticipated. A "partnering honouring" approach to a relationship is the one that involves the establishment of genuine friendship that allows an opportunity to explore each partner's character, background, and spiritual commitment as vital elements for something beyond friendship. Scripture and history from the books of Gen. 2:24; Matt. 19:6 indicate that marriage has three distinct characteristics:

- Permanency *("let no one separate")*
- Exclusivity *("leave, leave"), and*
- Conjugality *(husband and wife "shall become one flesh")*

For those who believe in the gospel, it is without a doubt that honouring God in a relationship is a sure way to honour a partner. It is not so difficult to find people trying to build a relationship through social media (Facebook, WhatsApp, Twitter, etc.) When an emotional attachment is established on social media between a man and a woman leading to marriage without deepened commitment, the relationship will not have the necessary structures to stand the test of time. The result will in no doubt reflect frustration, disappointment, and hurt unless the parties give each other the needed time to grow in understanding and learning to differentiate between love and lust; and charisma and character. An increasingly sexualised dating culture in modern society does not seemingly focus on establishing friendship and the exploration and discovery of relevant character, faithfulness habits, and conflict resolution abilities that contribute to stable marriages. Our popular dating system does not in most instances have support from family, church, or community leaders for significant input and direction.

But, How Do You Date and Honour God?

The bible only talks about "brother and sister" or "husband and wife". There's not really some middle place that our contemporary culture calls "dating". The sure way to honour God, as difficult as it may sound is to spend time treating each other with purity as brother and sister. Remember, you have no claim of anybody's life when you are dating him/her. It is surprising to see men of God and religious fanatics at the centre of abusive relationships when religious teachings have explicit directions against them. One of the widely used words in Christianity is glory, but few show proper understanding of it nor apply its real meaning to their relationships. There is no clear-cut direct instruction on dating in the Holy Book of Quran but if we want to Glorify God, then we have to learn to respect each other's boundaries.

Our motivation to dating should transcend being "moral animals" just to get attached to our partners to achieve our romantic goals. We must act on our moral values and use them as a constant guide to glorify our partners. A critical scenario is seen in the motivation for athletes when running a race. An athlete always has the finishing line in mind and once his/her objective of crossing the finishing line is achieved, there is no further motivation to proceed. If you put on the coat of moral values only to woe a partner to acceptance to fulfil a need, you will have no motivation to respect and glorify the person thereafter. Setting and respecting boundaries with a strong motivation to not cross them during dating is a recipe for maturity and self-discipline that instils respect and eternal glorification of dating leading to relationship and marriage that stands the test of time.

Two people may sometimes differ in what they believe in regarding physical boundaries, religious beliefs, or other life issues but if you are bound to glorify your partner, you will always embrace the change and differences to glorify each other. How we honour the people around us, especially in dating, will reveal if we are responding to love as demonstrated through the gospel of grace or we are just responding to infatuation and lust. You can honour the person you are dating by honouring their time, commitments, talents, opinions, and families. Honouring a person involves discovering ways to serve them and not be consumed by only your needs but the good of others. You are at liberty to do anything but not everything is worth doing, so date to get married. Casual dating might be popular and easier in this century, but if you're trying to achieve a sustainable long-term goal, then you should be looking for a spousal partner. Only date someone if you see them as a potential life-long partner. It doesn't therefore mean that you should marry the first person you date, of course not, but you have to spend quality time critically evaluating whether the person in question is a good fit for you or not. For instance, you should compare your values and long-term goals to ensure you're compatible.

There are couples with great relationships that are admirable and there are those that will make you feel like never committing yourself to anyone. Those great relationships are possible because there is a constant honour in all manner of ways. If you want to join the elite group of highly successful couples, let your partner know that they are valued in all the most meaningful ways. When you master the art of honouring your partner you directly honour God in the process and that breeds blessings into the union.

Consider the following points:

- *Cultivate self-discipline and desist from using hostility, criticism, judgment, or other forms of manipulation to get your way.*
- *Learn how to handle disappointment, anger, frustration, and resentment in a responsible way to avoid bruising your relationship unnecessarily*
- *Show respect and listen attentively when your partner speaks to you so that you don't misconstrue issues to cause unnecessary friction and misunderstanding.*
- *Hold yourselves as committed friends who will be each other's strongest support during difficult times.*
- *Understand that people change with time, as so do the needs of a relationship. Be flexible, adaptable, and creative about transitioning with changes that come with growth.*
- *Pick the right time to argue*
- *Avoid becoming physically intimate before you are convinced of a commitment or marriage*

Honouring doesn't mean you are always going to agree. Healthy disagreement is good but becomes toxic when you refuse to listen to anyone else leading to trouble.

As you consider establishing a culture of honour in our lives and all areas of influence, your true focus will be on honouring God and that will lead to a fulfilling relationship with your selves.

22

PHUBBING
(Phone Snubbing)

Many may be wondering what this term means because it's not common in our vocabulary. It was coined by an Australian advertising agency in 2012 to describe the growing phenomenon of people ignoring their friends and family who were right in front of them and instead of scrolling through their phones. Phubbing is simply the act of snubbing someone you're talking with in person in favour of your phone. I must say, I like many have been guilty of this act without necessarily acknowledging how much it affects relationships. While the behaviour in itself might not seem like a big deal, research suggests that it may be hurting your relationships and your mental health. One may ask, so how does it affect a relationship? Phubbing interrupts your ability to be present and engage with people around you. It directly makes personal face-to-face interactions less satisfying and can sometimes lead to irritation.

This problem may be getting worse because almost all adults own a cell phone for purposes of communication. Phubbing and the use of can badly impact a relationship can even instigate divorce because it decreases marital satisfaction with time. Gone were the days when our parent's only means of communication were through the exchange of letters which takes weeks and months to arrive at the recipient and several more weeks to receive a reply. The one thing that caught the attention of couples was the radio, for which both take a listen and talks to each other in the process. Today, in the advancement of technology and the availability of hi-tech communication mediums and 5G's, we are distracted by many things that put a strain on the needed attention required to nourish relationships through face-to-face communication.

The cell phone beeps and rings non-stop in very important bonding sessions with families, and even interrupts quality time with kids too. Conflicts over phone use are the driving force of many issues arising in relationships. A study published in the Journal of Applied Social Psychology found that people who viewed simulated snubbing felt more negatively about the interaction when they were told to imagine being the person phubbed than when they were not asked that. Constant use of the cell phone has become a real threat to fundamental human mental needs such as belongingness, self-esteem, meaningful existence, and control. Human beings are created with a characteristic to remain attuned to others, especially our partners. Thus, when we think that someone (especially our partner) isn't giving us their full attention, we feel disregarded and disrespected. When you're on your phone, it gives the impression that you're prioritizing something or someone else over your partner and that is where the problem starts from.

How do you feel when you are snubbed? You may feel unimportant and rejected and that alone can have a significant impact on your mental health. Social media has in a way made the situation worse because of its level of addiction. Being addicted to social media can easily cause depression and anxiety. Checking your phone, again and again, can become an impulse difficult to control. Ironically, your phone is meant to connect you, presumably, with someone through social media or texting but can severely disrupt your present moment, in face-to-face relationships. Series of studies have also shown that just having a phone out and present during a conversation interferes with your sense of connection to the other person, the feelings of closeness, and the quality of the conversation.

When we are on our phones, we are taken away from looking at other people and unable to read their facial expressions. We are unable to detect the nuances in their tone of voice (shaky with anxiety) or notice their body posture to ascertain if they are slumped and sad or excited and enthusiastic. But why do people get into these habits in the first place?

Fear of missing out *(FOMO)*, lack of self-control, and addiction to social media are the major culprits of this act. Decades of research have explicitly attested to the fact that our greatest need besides food and shelter is positive social connections with other human species. We are social creatures for whom connection and a sense of belonging are an integral part of our health and happiness. Given our nature, we involuntarily seek connection on social media at the cost of face-to-face opportunities for true intimacy with close associates or partners.

How Do I Stop Phubbing?

Making stopping a priority is the foremost step to success in this case. This means that mindfulness and self-awareness should be your non-negotiable priority. While you may not be able to control the behaviour of other people, you have a greater opportunity to model something different on your own through self-control. With that in mind, take note of the following as you journey through your transition period to start connecting:

Don't allow electronic communication to take precedence over face-to-face Interactions

Numerous researches suggest that, one of the very best things you can do for both your mental and physical health is to build strong social relationships, and those relationships we have in person are more intimate and connected. It is common knowledge that activities that involve other people do have positive effects on our mental health. At the end of the day, face-to-face social interactions tend to improve our mood and reduce depression than being glued electronically.

Initiate No Phone Zones

Parents, couples, and friends can decide to spend specific times together without the use of cell phones. An interesting but equally important thing to do is to create a technology-free room in the home—such as a living room or kitchen—where no phones or other devices are allowed.

Mute Notifications

Cell phone sounds automatically trigger the compulsion to check the phone, especially for those who are chronically dependent on their devices. It's easier to forget about the phone if it does not alert us to a message, email, and updates during face-to-face discussions.

Leave Your Phone Behind

Make it a point to leave your phone behind when going into a conversation with a partner or group. It might not be easy, but don't be scared to simply leave your phone in the car, desk drawer, or bag for some time. After all, whatever alerts you missed will be waiting for you to respond at a later time.

Excuse Yourself to Use Your Phone

If you are compelled to make use of your phone at any point in time during interactions, make it a habit to excuse yourself from the conversation or group in a manner that will not feel like you are snubbing the people you are in conversation with.

But Wait, What Do You Do When You Are the One Being Phubbed?

Immediately put on your armour of patience and compassion as the key to dealing with the situation. You will have to come to the understanding that the phubber is not necessarily doing it with malicious intent, but rather responding to an impulse to connect. Their goal like that of yourself or any other person might not be to exclude, but might rather be fishing out for inclusion.

A scary study indicates that for every minute we spend online for leisure, we don't just compromise our relationships, but we also lose valuable self-care time (e.g. sleep, household activities) and productivity. The less time on the phone, the more time available for meaningful conversations that will ultimately benefit our mental health and our sense of connection and belonging. As a matter of friendly caution, the next time you're with another person whether a partner or not, and you feel tempted to pull out your phone—stop and think again. Phubbing is a learned behaviour like any other habit you can relate to. The good thing is that you can unlearn any learned behaviour that develops into a habit. It will take some time and some pretty much sacrifices, but your mental health and your relationships will thank you for it.

23

"CREEPY LOVE" *GENDER-BASED VIOLENCE*

Gender-Based Violence is self-defined and one that is easily understood by any person. It is commonly witnessed tearing society apart and robbing the world of individuals who could shape this world of great uncertainties. The United Nations Population Fund defines it as violence against women and girls and one of the most prevalent human rights violations in the world. This is violence that knows no social, economic, or national boundaries. It's nerve breaking to accept the reality that, an estimated one in three women will experience physical or sexual abuse in their life around the globe.

But what exactly inspires violence leading to permanent emotional or physical damage or death? A lot of theories have been argued for and against it but the reality is that any action that causes unbearable harm to another person is simply inhuman and must be condemned by all sense and purpose. The expectations associated with different genders vary from one society to the other over time. The structures of patriarchal power dominate in many societies where male leadership is seen as the norm, and men therefore hold the majority of power. Patriarchy is seemingly a social and political system that unfortunately treats men as superior to women. Women at the very least are unable to neither protect their bodies and meet their basic needs nor fully participate in societal activities, leaving them at the mercy of men to perpetrate violence with impunity against them. Interestingly, population-based surveys show very high levels of intimate partner violence (IPV) and non-partner sexual violence (SV) in particular, with IPV being the most common form of violence against women. The sickening part is the violence reported from intimate partners but those from non-partner sexual violence are equally animalistic.

Why do I say so? How do you inflict pain on a person you claim to love, and how do you make love to someone who does not have the same sexual consent as you? What's the essence of sex if it's not for both parties to reach a level of satisfaction in agreement? There seem to be more questions than answers when the issue of GBV is raised because it's very difficult to understand what goes on in the minds of the abusers and the abused altogether. But one certain thing is that someone gets hurt in the process and that alone makes it wrong without any justification. Sometimes, we are tempted to ask why the abused don't leave the abuser, but the most dangerous time for an abused woman is when she attempts to leave her abuser. Some women opt to stay for some time because of their strong believe that they could keep the family together. Some women are also sometimes blamed for the violence and are coerced to stay by immediate family and friends. Others stay because they are financially dependent on their partner and they get torn between choices of poverty and violence.

Domestic abuse which happens to be the first son of GBV is often a gradual process occurrence. The frequency of assaults and seriousness of the violence escalates with time and not at once. Abusers in most cases express deep remorse with a promise to change making it difficult for women to come to the point of realising that, the violence will never stop and that the relationship is unsalvageable. The path of realisation is often reached late and the long-term experience of being abused eventually destroys the woman's self-confidence, making it more difficult for her to believe that she deserves better in life. Women then lose the courage to leave believing that they cannot manage life on their own. One of the most serious setbacks to GBV is the fact that a section of society does not take violence against women seriously and sees it as a 'private matter between the couple. Such attitude must be confronted and changed.

Children who are witnesses to GBV are the most unfortunate ones because the memory of what they experience might be taken out of context or misread in different forms and shapes.

This is what makes those who witness such abuse easily fall victim to GBV or grow to become abusers themselves. GBV occurs across the life cycle, from early childhood to the final years of life. From an early age in their homes, schools, and other institutional settings, children are exposed to societal norms, social cues, and attitudes about gender roles that shape how they perceive others and value themselves. By the time children enter the gate of schools for their first grade, many of the collective messages from these experiences and attitudes have already taken hold of them.

To promote positive behaviours and engage everyone directly in stopping GBV, we need to focus our attention on equipping people with better tools to navigate dating, relationships, and different environments in a safe manner. We need to embraces strategies to transform culture, combat bias, and foster inclusion. And this should start right from our homes with the young ones before they grow into teen ages and adulthood. This is because the prevalence of GBV among young people follows them into adulthood and early education will equally lead them to understand and become responsible adults that will see violence as a menace to society and not a norm. GBV does not dissipate over time; rather, it extends to the other side of the age spectrum. Elderly women face the majority of elder abuse, where some of them are tagged as witches and wizards and all bad deeds in society are attributed to their doings. It's sad to note that abuse of elders in society is mostly perpetrated by relatives, spouses, or adult children who in most cases act as primary caregivers.

We often look at violence in intimate relationships when GBV is discussed but it also occurs across many different types of relationships including personal ones, those that are professional and work-based to more informal or one-time interactions. Intimate Partner Violence on the one hand often involves a power dynamic within a relationship that manifests itself in different forms of control or coercion outside of physical abuse that can deepen the long-term effects of GBV for women.

The abusers' strategies often stem from exerting control to dictate every aspect of the relationship, from economic decisions to decisions about starting a family or becoming involved in civic or community activities. One common economic abuse is when an abuser controls or limits a woman's financial independence and their ability to work or engage in economic activities. Abusers also easily interfere with the reproduction autonomy of women by the use of intimidation of threats to either make a woman fall pregnant or not fall pregnant or even put pressure on some women to terminate the pregnancy.

GBV can also involve acquaintances such as casual friends, neighbours, or a stranger. The occurrence of GBV outside of intimate relationships is a stark reminder that the misuse and abuse of power are not limited to private relationships but power imbalances are broadly used in a variety of contexts to control women and gender minorities and to undermine them. If you are in love with your abuser, then that is a bit confusing and should be a painful ordeal. One of two things may be possible if you found yourself in love with your abuser. You may fear for your sanity, your sense of identity, and possibly even your life on the one hand, and you may be clinging to a loose straw of times your partner is loving and thoughtful, and that creates the feeling that you're loved enough not to leave.

It beats imagination how people thrive in abusive relationships but if you consider that most abusers are nice, charming, and attentive at first, it becomes easy to see how "love" often thrives in abusive situations. Your reason for holding onto the relationship even though you are being abused is to simply desire to feel safe again and again after each incident of abuse. That is why you believe your abuser when he says he loves you and it will never happen again. It is imperative to note that, our primitive minds do not always factor in our need for long-term safety; they only see the danger as it occurs. Be mindful therefore that, staying in an abusive relationship out of love or for whatever reason will not protect you and it will not make you the happiest person.

Trust me to say that, in almost all relationships of this kind, the abuse only gets worse and dangerous over time. It's very easy for anyone to say the words "I love you," what is not easy is the act of the feeling of "love" in its true sense. Love is not enough reason to stay at the hands of an abuser. Love is built on mutual respect; trust, and good communication, therefore neither physical nor emotional abuse should have a seat at the table when love is being served.

You will have to take a good look at your relationship again if you are the type that often finds it easy agreeing with an abuser after a fight or begins to see things from an abuser's point of view. Know that your action is simply a coping mechanism where you detach yourself from your pain or fear to cope with the situation in the interim. At this point, as you detach, you may even take on certain aspects of your partner's personality or even fall more in love with the abuser all over again which is what you feel he needs. Such actions might temporarily appease your abuser's ego which may temporarily stop you from getting hurt and even ignite a loving response back and forth. Disconnecting and absorbing responsibility all in the hope of fixing the abuse is a natural state of action.

Continuously staying with your abuser feels like love but that is far from what love is meant to be. I have heard people say that a relationship can withstand anything as long as there's love but that is not true. I am not casting doubt on the fact that your abuser loved the only way he knew how, and you may love him too, but all these supposed shared feelings do not stop him from abusing, insulting, devaluing, and inflicting pain on you. That kind of love is irrational and the earlier you take a step towards an escape the better. Keep in mind that, being in love with your abuser won't stop him from hurting you over and over again, so advice yourself and preserve your love to those who will value it.

One of the many misconceptions about abusive men is that they have anger issues. I beg to defer here because these people don't go around beating their bosses, colleagues all other people they meet on the street when provoked but have the audacity to use their supposed loved one's face as a punching bag.

They abuse their partners consciously and use physical violence just to stay in control. It is also a myth to assume that abusers genuinely love the women they beat. They are only obsessed with their partners and that leads them to jealousy and controlling as they do not have what it takes to love. Abusive men rarely do it once so if you're in a relationship with a guy who has pushed, hit, or slapped you once or twice, take it as a warm-up to series of worse events yet to unfold. You can always expect them to do it again and again. Not all abusive relationships involve physical violence. The fact that you are not battered and bruised doesn't mean you're not being abused. Unfortunately, emotional abuse is often minimized, overlooked, or underestimated even by the person experiencing it. Emotional abuse is directed to chip away at your feelings of self-worth and independence. It leaves you feeling that there's no way out of the relationship and that you are nothing without your abusive partner.

Spotting an Abuser

One question I have been asked several times is "how can an abuser be identified"? Seems like an easy question to answer but I can understand why lots of people seek clarification and answers to this simple but difficult to conceptualise question. This is because abusers are in most cases lovers or immediate family members or friends to the abused. Numerous women are interested in ways to spot a potential abuser, especially once they have been involved in an abusive relationship. The more signs a person has, the more likely the person is an abuser. In some cases, an abuser may have only a few behaviours that the woman can recognize, but people mistakenly try to explain the behaviour as a sign of love and concern.

Jealousy

Lots of people defend their act of jealousy by saying that it is a sign of love. Well, I don't think Jealousy has anything to do with love; rather it is an indication of possessiveness and lack of trust.

Abusers may in most cases question their partners about who they hand out with and why. As time progresses, a potential abuser will accuse you of flirting or possibly having an affair. He may call intermittently to in guise as a caring partner during the day or drop by uninformed. Abusers may out of jealousy refuse to let their partners work for fear they might meet someone else at the place of work. They could even go to the extent of asking friends to check you out.

Isolation

An abuser can go to the extent of calling you names like whore if you are seen with male friends and a lesbian if you associate with female friends. They do that to coerce you mentally to isolate you from all necessary contacts. To achieve isolating you, they can even deprive you of basic resources such as cell phones if not they will monitor your activities and appearances on social media to be in the know of your movement and interactions.

Blames Others for Problems and Is Good at Denying

If there is one thing abusers are good at, it is blaming others for every mistake of their life. They will blame you and will be quick at stating how actions upset them and made it impossible for them to achieve a certain goal or to concentrate on a task as expected. They could even go to the extent of blaming their actions on external circumstances such as a bad day or their childhood. Anyone can be an abuser and they also come from all walks of life, cultures, religions, economic levels, races, etc.

Abusers can be your neighbour, pastor, friend, child's teacher, relative, co-worker, and just anyone who exhibits signs of being an abuser. It is important to note that majority of abusers do not have criminal records and are generally law-abiding outside of the home. Abusers cannot be said to have one typical, detectable personality of but they do often display common characteristics.

The following are red flags:

Previous Abusive Behaviour

Abusers admit their past deviant behaviours but are quick to blame it on their ex-partners with cooked-up excuses to justify their actions.

Use of Force during Misunderstanding and Argument

This happens by preventing you from leaving his sight or the premises from which the argument ensued. They may go to the point of pushing or shoving you here and there

Rough and Unpleasant Sex Roles

Abusers see women as inferior and use them to in most cases satisfy their sexual needs. They expect you to obey them in all instances even if the act for which you are forced to undertake is against your will or beliefs. They force you to play bedroom roles as though you are a porn star regardless of how you feel.

Intimidation

They use intimidation is as a tactic to scare their victims through gestures, violent actions (such as smashing things), or threats to hurt the victim's loved ones.

Selective On Whom to Abuse

One thing worth noting is that abusers do not abuse everyone around them; instead, they are very selective with who they target. They will put on their sheep clothes with some people and appear completely normal to everyone but their victim. They can stop their abusive behaviour if they choose to do so and when it is not in their interests to act normal.

24

ANCIENT PROVERBIAL EXPRESSION OF WISDOM

Our predecessors often used short expressions of popular wisdom to narrate a story, illustrate ideas, and deliver messages of inspiration. The wisdom in such short and simple statements cannot be overlooked in our generation. A treasure of wisdom has been handed down to us in the form of proverbs that if well understood can motivate and shape our lives in so many ways. Many wise men have stated that we cannot understand the present without truthfully acknowledging the past. There is a global awakening of deceit and unhealthy relationships that appear to be marked with abuse and conflicted beliefs that leads to sporadic divorce and bitter break-ups and loss of friends. You can draw some inspiration from these timeless proverbs of the past because when you follow in the path of your father, you learn to walk like him. Our predecessors undoubtedly had fewer break-ups and divorces than we currently experience. They built their relationships on a foundation of in-depth understanding of life and the moral values of the world around them.

Proverbs always awake my interest as I believe they provide an insightful opportunity into a community of lifestyle, history and People all over the continent in one way or the other make use of proverbial statements and quotes to communicate to their family, friends, and acquaintances including love ones. Below is a collection of proverbial words of wisdom from specific countries across the globe that will challenge your thoughts. Think deeply of such statements and deliberate on their meanings while you try to incorporate them into your daily conversation.

America

Beauty is only skin deep, which means a pleasant appearance is not a guide to character. It is imperative to remain careful when choosing a friend, an acquaintance, or anyone as a significant partner towards commitment. Outward beauty can be seriously misleading. If you rely on the outside beauty of a partner you will be disappointed during your relationship because beauty is only on the surface but the real beauty is far beyond the sight of the human eye. It takes something much more than the eye to see the beauty of a person.

Spanish

Whoever gossips to you will gossip about you, which means that if someone is quick at gossiping to you, chances are that they will gossip about you too. Be careful who you share your secrets with. Some friends will say all sorts of negative things about your partner or other partners in a relationship. Such people may equally say similar negative things about you to other people in your absence. Never feed on gossip as it may sooner or later lead to the destruction of your relationship.

English

Beauty lies in the eye of the beholder, this basically means that, we don't have the same opinions about what is beautiful and not. The observer is the one that determines what is beautiful to him/her. In as much as other people can attest to the beauty of specific individuals whom you are also attracted to, the point of attraction may differ from one person to the other. Five men may have five different reasons why they are attracted to a specific female and vice versa. At the end of the day, you are the only one that knows and understand the reason behind what you consider beautiful or not.

French

Good advice is often annoying; bad advice never is. Meaning, you won't always hear what you want to hear. You will find it difficult to correct yourself if you are always around people who say "yes" to everything you ask or do. Most often than not, we are comfortable around people that will give us advice that confirms our thoughts than those that will tell us something opposite to our assumptions. We seek not the truth about the confirmation of our expectations. Be careful of a partner who sees nothing wrong with you and does not stand against your waywardness.

Arab

Examine what is said, not who speaks. Therefore, don't easily judge people by their looks. Appearance is important but should not be the sole purpose for which the value of something is judged. Don't judge people based on their past or situation or you risk ignoring important information. Be circumspect in the receiving of information from people and analyse what is being said rather than the one saying it.

Greek

The heart that loves is always young. Truly that when you love you become like a child and not childish. This is because children have pure feelings of thoughts, easily forgives and their heart is always young. Having a loving heart gives you eternal freedom of peace compared to showing love with conditions. Conditional love makes you weary at all times and takes away your innermost joy and happiness.

Ghana

The one looking for a wife does not speak with contempt about women. *Meaning*, have a mind-set of disregarding and dismissing women because you don't value their opinions will chase away potential suitors. You cannot by all sense and purpose disrespect women and still expect one as a partner. A man who shows disrespect to one or two women will certainly show disrespect to others.

South Africa

Love, like rain, does not choose the grass on which it falls. *Meaning*, True love means what is mine is yours. When you love somebody, you love the person in totality and do not select which aspect of the person you want to dedicate yourself to. Some people only love their partners because of some material expectation or sex.

Sudan

If nakedness promises you a piece of cloth, ask him his name. *Means*: be careful of people that make promises to you It is impossible for a person without clothes to promise you clothing. Some people will promise you heaven and earth to get into a relationship to satisfy their selfish end. Scrutinise every promise and find out if the person making them is capable of delivering.

Nigeria

The man who says he will not marry a woman with admirers will never marry. *Means*: Every woman is in one way or the other admired by another. Human beings don't stop admiring other humans because they are married. You cannot blame your spouse for being admired by other people as long as it does not lead to sexual promiscuity.

Morocco

Do not correct with a strike that which can be taught with a kiss. *Stipulating* that, by all means try not to hit someone for the least provocations. It makes no sense to lay hands on a spouse for a wrongful act. You can correct your spouse in modesty without necessary being physical.

Kenya

If you laugh at your mother-in-law, you will get dirt in your eyes. *Meaning*, laughing at your in-laws will make you see no good in them. It is considered utter disrespect to make fun of a mother-in-law. Who will you go to if you have a problem with your hubby? Mothers-in-law are our mothers from an African cultural context and needed to be accorded the same respect we give to our biological parents.

Ethiopia

A woman married without consultation runs away without consultation. *Means*: dating a woman without proper marital procedures paves way for her to leave at her will. It is only proper for a man to get married to a woman before staying with her as a partner. Cohabitation does not guarantee stability and a partner will leave the relationship as and when they do not benefit without any hint whatsoever.

Egypt

If you marry a monkey for his wealth, the money goes and the monkey remains as is. *Means*: if you marry a man or woman due to material possessions, you will face the reality of which you are married to when in the absence of those goodies. It is dangerous to be married to a person because of their possessions or a specific need. The absence of that need for which the relationship was built will mean the end of the relationship. Marriage of convenience is a recipe for disaster as the real character and personalities of people manifest themselves in due time.

Burundi

Where there is love there is no darkness. *Means*: Love gives way to freedom and overcomes all adversities. Genuine love makes all things possible. Where there is true love there is forgiveness and couples do not hold each other's mistakes against themselves. No partner will inflict pain onto you nor hold grudges against you forever because love overcomes all darkness and faults.

Algeria

A sensible enemy is better than a narrow-minded friend. *Means*: a person who tells you the truth of your acts though painful is a good companion than a friend who approves all your dealings regardless of whether you are wrong or right. Make friends with people who can positively impact your life and relationships and not those who will mislead you by blindly supporting you.

Liberia

When a crazy man runs away with your clothes while you are in the bathroom, don't follow him. *Means:* do not allow people to mislead you by doing things because others are doing it too. Don't follow irrational people for irrational things. If you run after a crazy man to take the clothes he/she took from you while bathing, you will be out naked on the street and people will not be able to differentiate between you and the crazy man. Do not allow yourself into fighting useless battles. Learn to disregard people who try to lure you into doing the unexpected.

Madagascar

Don't be so much in love that you can't tell when it's raining. *Means*: do not lose your mind because of love. Love is good but doesn't lose yourself when you are in love, else you risk being fooled into a pool of disappointment and hurt. There has been an instance when people remain in relationships flouted with untold abuse and insist on absorbing everything that comes to them in the name of love. Such people are drunk in love and can't tell when it is raining. Be in love but always remain sane to understand times and seasons.

Zimbabwe

God is good but never dance with a lion. *Means*: remember to take a calculated risk at all times. Use your mind and don't involve yourself in dreadful situations believing that someone will save you. In as much as God will see you through all situations including that of your relationship; be careful not to be deliberately engaged in a relationship or marriage with a person that you perfectly know possesses a bad attitude or character with a believe that God will change the person.

African-Americans

If you are wise and seek to make your house stable, love your wife fully and righteously. *Means*: unconditional love is the mark of a good marriage. You cannot wish for a stable marriage home without loving your family and standing up for them.

Tanzania

Do not make the dress before the child is born. Means: Do not make promises you are not sure to fulfil or exercise patient to know the real context of an issue before acting. In the olden days when there was no ultrasound scan to determine the gender of babies before birth, our mothers had to wait for their children to be born before buying clothes to avoid buying the wrong ones. It is, therefore, necessary to exercise patient for confirmation before making decisions to avoid regrets.

Gabon

If the needle doesn't pass the thread doesn't follow. *Means*: attend to primary issues before attempting secondary issues. First things first. It is much easier to do things the right way by following due process. Whenever you are faced with difficulties as to which choice to make in a given situation, remember to always handle the primary issues first before attempting secondary issues.

CONCLUSION

Relationships are about communication, and all communication, including prayer, is a two-way process that is and will always be important in human existence. The value of human relationships is so much a part of humanity that we can hardly live without it because we rely on the strength of human relationships to survive and thrive. Healthy relationships are the foundations upon which happy and productive lives are built. The central role that relationships play in the lives of people around the globe makes it necessary for a systematic study and discussions to uncover that which builds thriving and flourishing relationships and families. It is my strongest belief that flourishing families and relationships are capable elements that will lead to flourishing societies.

On the other hand, broken families and relationships have the potential to greatly deter personal and societal growth and peace. There are certainly many topics to uncover but the ones we have dealt with here can be a catalyst to inspire everyone to be mindful of life and issues surrounding relationships through proper understanding and descriptions.

Understanding the formation and true essence of a relationship will go a long way to reduce Gender-Based Violence to a point where perpetrators will be transformed to the good of society through knowledge and understanding. I am eternally convinced that, if we give value to our romantic and personal relationships with a true understanding of why we specifically relate to our friends, partners, and family members, we will be filled with true love that will overcome setbacks that breeds pain and even untimely death of many.

This collection of life and relationship probing issues that have been carefully dissected is aimed at providing readers with a fine understanding to enhance healthy relationship amongst the high-graded species of all creations (human beings). Knowledge is power and the lack of it is detrimental to the very existence of man in this dynamic world.

-The End-

www.ingramcontent.com/pod-product-compliance
Lightning Source LLC
LaVergne TN
LVHW051058080426
835508LV00019B/1940